Test Your English Vocabulary

in Use

Upper-intermediate

with answers

Second Edition

Felicity O'Dell
Michael McCarthy

CAMBRIDGE
UNIVERSITY PRESS

CAMBRIDGE
UNIVERSITY PRESS

University Printing House, Cambridge CB2 8BS, United Kingdom

One Liberty Plaza, 20th Floor, New York, NY 10006, USA

477 Williamstown Road, Port Melbourne, VIC 3207, Australia

314–321, 3rd Floor, Plot 3, Splendor Forum, Jasola District Centre,
New Delhi – 110025, India

79 Anson Road, #06–04/06, Singapore 079906

Cambridge University Press is part of the University of Cambridge.

It furthers the University's mission by disseminating knowledge in the pursuit of
education, learning and research at the highest international levels of excellence.

www.cambridge.org
Information on this title: www.cambridge.org/9781107638785

First published 2012

Printed in Great Britain by CPI Group (UK) Ltd, Croydon CR0 4YY

A catalogue record for this publication is available from the British Library

ISBN 978-1107-60094-2 English Vocabulary in Use Upper-intermediate with
Answers and CD-ROM
ISBN 978-1107-63878-5 Test Your English Vocabulary in Use Upper-intermediate

Contents

Acknowledgements

We are very grateful to all the schools, institutions, teachers and students around the world who piloted or commented on the material. We would also like to thank our editors at Cambridge and, in particular, Janet Weller for her thorough and thoughtful work on the project. Janet contributed a great deal to the contents of these tests.

Photo Acknowledgements

The authors and publishers acknowledge the following sources of copyright material and are grateful for the permissions granted. While every effort has been made, it has not always been possible to identify the sources of all the material used, or to trace all copyright holders. If any omissions are brought to our notice, we will be happy to include the appropriate acknowledgements on reprinting.

p. 8 (CL, BL & TR), 14 (R) and 37 (TL): Thinkstock; p. 8 (BR): Shutterstock/3drenderings; p. 14 (L) Thinkstock/Stockbyte; p. 14 (CL): Thinkstock/Jupiter Images; p. 14 (C): Thinkstock/ Photodisk; p. 14 (CR): Shutterstock/Felix Mizioznikov; p. 35 (TL) Shutterstock/chubphong; p. 35 (TCL, BL & BC): Shutterstock/hkannn; p. 37 (TR): Shutterstock; p. 37 (C): Shutterstock/ Liusa; p. 37 (CR): Shutterstock/hypnotype; p. 39 (3): Shutterstock/MrGarry; p. 39 (4): Shutterstock/Nemeziya; p. 39 (5): Shutterstock/Oleksiy Mark.

Introduction

Why test vocabulary?

Research has shown that you usually need to meet a word at least seven times before you know it properly. Doing exercises like these, practising words and expressions that you have already encountered, is a useful way of helping you to fix the words you have been studying in your long-term memory.

What vocabulary is tested?

This book provides a series of tests of English vocabulary at upper-intermediate level. It is based on the vocabulary presented and practised in *English Vocabulary in Use: Upper-intermediate*. There is a test corresponding to each unit of that book. You can, of course, also use this book if you have not been working with *English Vocabulary in Use* but are simply interested in assessing your knowledge of the vocabulary area covered by the test.

How do I score my tests?

Each test is scored out of 35, and a key, containing information about how many marks each item gets, is included at the back of the book. It should be clear from the key what you need to write to get each mark and so you should be able to score your work without a teacher, if you wish to.

The first exercise in each test always offers a maximum score of 10 and it is recommended that you do this exercise first. If your score for this exercise is less than 5, then we suggest that you do a bit more work in the language area covered by the test before doing the rest of it.

Although the tests are all scored out of 35, you will probably feel that some tests are easier than others. This is partly because everyone is more familiar with some vocabulary areas than others. However, because certain vocabulary areas are particularly dense, occasionally you will need to show that you know more words and expressions than you would need to in order to get the same score in other tests.

How long do the tests take?

Each test should take 20 to 30 minutes to complete.

We hope that you enjoy using these tests and that they will help you to learn the vocabulary that you want and need to master at this level.

Learning vocabulary

1.1
10 marks

Match the collocations.

Example ~~rich~~ vocabulary.

(~~rich~~) (a sense) (a train) (palace) (a phrase) (set)

(at a loss) (common) (a remarkable) (~~vocabulary~~) (sides) (for words)

(to coin) (a subtle) (to take) (coincidence) (sense)

(a royal) (to express) (difference) (of humour) (an opinion)

1.2
5 marks

Match the organs of the body with their functions.

Example liver | b |

1 lungs | | a pumps blood round your body
2 intestines | | b cleans the body and produces bile
3 heart | | c digestion of food starts here
4 kidneys | | d remove waste and produce urine
5 stomach | | e you breathe with these
                          f long tubes which take food through the body

1.3
5 marks

Choose the correct answers to the questions.

Example Which letter in *subtle* is silent? (b)/ t / l

1 Which noun is only used in the plural? *scissors, fish, crumbs*
2 Which word does NOT mean a grammatical part of speech? *noun, verb, adjective, text*
3 Which word does NOT have a silent letter? *lamb, answer, express, debt*
4 In which word does *ch* sound like *k*? *church, chemist, child, chicken*
5 Which of these words is more formal than the others? *to alight, to feel gutted, awesome, to bug someone*

1.4
5 marks

Complete the labels.

Example ( ) circle

1 | | r _ _ _ _ _ _ _   4 [image] s _ _ _ _ _ _ _
2 [image] s _ _ _ _ _ _ _ _ _ _   5 [image] c _ _ _
3 [image] c _ _ _

1.5
10 marks

Put the words from the box in the correct columns.

| ~~TV~~ blogs audio books magazines songs DVDs tweets encyclopedias recipes podcasts comics |

things you can read	things you can watch / listen to
	TV

Organising a vocabulary notebook

2.1 Decide if each underlined word or phrase is: a noun, a verb, an adjective, a fixed
phrase or a collocation.

Example I love <u>spicy</u> food. *adjective*

1 George can sit there <u>strumming</u> his guitar for hours on end.
2 We had a very <u>productive</u> meeting yesterday.
3 No one here <u>earns</u> a particularly high salary.
4 Are you <u>in a hurry</u> to leave?
5 I don't know Fatima well – she's just a <u>casual</u> acquaintance.
6 Do you prefer <u>classical</u> or pop music?
7 You can buy <u>fresh farm produce</u> every day at the market.
8 After the long day's trek through the rainforest, I soon fell into a <u>deep sleep</u>.
9 Our journey here was an absolute <u>nightmare</u>!
10 You can <u>count on</u> Eli to help out in an emergency.

2.2 Put the words and expressions from the box into the most appropriate network.

~~piano~~   blog   the web   cello   identity theft   folk   social network
a track   upload a video   release an album

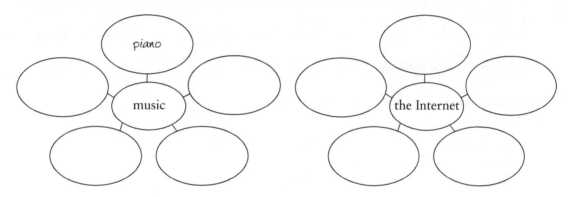

2.3 Are these pairs of words synonyms or antonyms? Write S (synonyms) or A (antonyms).

Example pleased, glad S

1 mild, spicy
2 win, gain
3 urban, rural
4 stop, cease

5 cold, chilly
6 supply with, deprive of
7 spam, junk mail
8 rush, dash

2.4 Complete the word formation table.

noun	verb	adjective
product, ...*produce*...	....	....
....	....	practical
politics, ...		....
....	....	informative

Using your dictionary

3.1
10 marks
These words are written in the IPA. Write the usual alphabet versions.

Example /ðæt/ ....*that*.........

1 /ə'mʌŋ/ ....
2 /tʃɜːtʃ/ ....
3 /'næʃənəl/ ....
4 /θɜː'tiːn/ ....
5 /'pleʒə/ ....

6 /'paːswɜːd/ ....
7 /'mʌðə/ ....
8 /'fæsɪneɪtɪŋ/ ....
9 /edʒʊ'keɪʃənəl/ ....
10 /ə'sliːp/ ....

3.2
9 marks
Which words are being defined?

Example words with similar meanings .....*synonyms*.....

1 a kind of verb that must have an object ....
2 how words characteristically go together ....
3 how a word is said ....
4 the word used to talk about which syllable has the most emphasis when a word is said ....
5 a kind of verb that doesn't need an object ....
6 a short form of a longer word ....
7 words with opposite meanings ....
8 a word used before a noun, noun phrase or pronoun, connecting it to another word, e.g. *with, in, from* ....
9 a word like *and, although* or *because* that connects two parts of a sentence ....

3.3
6 marks
Underline the stressed syllables in these words.

Example <u>el</u>egant

1 extract (noun)
2 supply
3 thermometer

4 lifestyle
5 record (verb)
6 record (noun)

3.4
10 marks
Correct the mistakes in these sentences.

Example I found the film absolutely ~~fascinated~~. *fascinating.*

1 The accused man denied to steal the car.
2 The college will supply you of a coursebook.
3 I suggest you to revise the first three units of this book before the test.
4 You shouldn't make such hurtfull remarks.
5 When are you going to get round to tidy your bedroom?

Your score

/35

4.1 Explain the meanings of the underlined words / phrases.

10 marks

Example The city centre is now a <u>car-free</u> zone. *cars are not allowed*

1 How can you be so <u>cold-hearted</u>?
2 The company has decided to <u>discontinue</u> its de luxe range.
3 Kate is <u>up to her ears</u> in work at the moment.
4 It was a scene of <u>unimaginable</u> devastation.
5 There was a large <u>anti-government</u> demonstration at the weekend.
6 I use my <u>bread-maker</u> almost every day.
7 They said they hadn't received my email and asked me to <u>resend</u> it.
8 The island has been <u>uninhabited</u> for some years now.
9 Both the bride and the groom are experiencing some <u>pre-wedding</u> nerves.
10 The creatures wake in March after a three-month period of <u>hibernation</u>.

4.2 Match the underlined words in the sentences to the most likely meanings in the box.

5 marks

> type of flower   type of bird   type of tool   type of movement
> type of laughing   ~~type of food~~

Example I'd like a large <u>macaroon</u> to have with my coffee please. *type of food*

1 The teacher looked up when she heard the girls at the back of the class <u>tittering</u>.
2 Jake used a big <u>saw</u> to cut down the tree.
3 There were some tall <u>delphiniums</u> in the border next to the garden gate.
4 As I watched, the snake <u>slithered</u> into the long grass.
5 The noise made me look up and I saw a colourful <u>woodpecker</u> perched on a high branch of a tall pine.

4.3 What do these compound nouns mean?

10 marks

Example a bicycle helmet *a helmet for a cyclist to wear*

1 a glasses case
2 a cat basket
3 a teaspoon
4 a bus lane
5 a footstool

6 a butter dish
7 an ice cream maker
8 a computer magazine
9 a bottle opener
10 a streetlight

4.4 Complete the sentences with words based on the words in brackets.

10 marks

Example A ....*bi-monthly*.... report is one which comes out every two months. (month)

1 Simon's being very .... with everyone today for some reason. (rat)
2 After such a long absence, I found the town almost .... (recognise)
3 The fields were full of carefully .... crops. (tend)
4 People from that area are well-known for their ...., with many surviving until 90 or 100. (long)
5 We have to .... the old gas cooker and they'll take it away when they deliver the new one. (connect)
6 .... people think it is bad luck to walk under a ladder. (superstition)
7 The average human .... is increasing in most countries. (span)
8 Payne's last novel was .... as he died before writing the final chapter. (finish)
9 Emily has a nut allergy so she can only eat cakes or biscuits if they're .... (nut)
10 I think you should .... the card before sending it, as you've made several spelling mistakes in it. (write)

Your score

/35

Countries, nationalities and languages

5.1
10 marks

Do these places need *the* in front of them? Put *the* or – .

Example ....–........ France

1 .... United Kingdom	6 .... Canada
2 .... Australia	7 .... USA
3 .... Arctic	8 .... Poland
4 .... Philippines	9 .... Argentina
5 .... India	10 .... United Arab Emirates

5.2
10 marks

Make nationality / cultural identity adjectives from these countries.

Example Pakistan ....*Pakistani*........

1 Japan	6 Iraq ....
2 Brazil	7 Denmark ....
3 Ireland	8 Turkey ....
4 Bangladesh	9 Iceland ....
5 Korea	10 Thailand ....

5.3
10 marks

Correct the mistakes in these sentences.

Example She went to ~~the~~ Russia on holiday.

1 I think she married a French.
2 Do you speak any Arab?
3 My sister was born in the Central East, in Jordan to be precise.
4 I plan to learn some Greece before I go to live in Athens.
5 Stand in this queue if you have an European passport.
6 I'd love to visit the Antarctica.
7 I met some very nice Finnish and Swedish on holiday.
8 Amsterdam is the capital of Netherlands, even though The Hague is the seat of government.
9 Columbus sailed across the Atlantic to Caribbean.
10 We had a wonderful holiday in the Switzerland mountains.

5.4
5 marks

What do we call ...

Example ... a person who comes from Israel? *an Israeli*

1 ... someone who only speaks one language? ....
2 ... someone who speaks many languages? ....
3 ... the language you learnt from your birth? ....
4 ... different forms of the same language? ....
5 ... a person who comes from Cyprus? ....

Your score

/35

6.1 Put the words from the box in the most appropriate columns.

10 marks

> boiling downpour flood freeze frost heatwave
> humid shower stifling thaw ~~torrential rain~~

cold weather	hot weather	wet weather
		torrential rain

6.2 Complete the sentences with the correct words. (The first letters are given.)

14 marks

Example We had to stay in Florida for a couple of extra days because the h*urricane*............ was
too bad for planes to be able to fly.

1 In spring the ice m............................, the snow t............................ and the plants start to grow again.
2 It was hot on the beach but there was a gentle b............................ that cooled us a little.
3 The sky is very o............................ – I think it's going to p............................ soon.
4 It's so hard to work in this hot, m............................ weather, isn't it!
5 Winters in this country are not normally as s............................ as they've been this year.
6 As there has been very little rain this year so far, people are beginning to worry about the
possibility of d............................ .
7 We don't often experience foggy days here, but it's sometimes a little m............................ in
the early mornings.
8 No one e............................ it still to be so warm in l............................ autumn.
9 The d............................ temperatures are quite warm but it can get cold at night.
10 The rain is very h............................ – I hope the river won't f............................ .

6.3 Which is the odd one out? Explain why.

6 marks

Example mild, tropical, warm, (chilly) *the other words refer to heat / warmth*

1 boiling, stifling, damp, muggy
2 drought, hurricane, gale, breeze
3 shower, frost, downpour, rain

6.4 Correct the mistakes in these sentences.

5 marks

Example It was a very ~~fog~~ day yesterday. *foggy*

1 The rain was so heavy that several roads got flood.
2 I haven't seen such torrent rain for a very long time.
3 There was such a strong windy that my mum's hat blew off.
4 Do you have to go out in this pourdown?
5 We had a very nice weather on our holiday.

Describing people: appearance

7.1
10 marks
Complete the descriptions of these people. (The first letters are given.)

1   2   3   4   5

1 He's r_ound_................-faced, b............................ and has dark s............................. .
2 She's got b............................ hair and is f............................-skinned.
3 She's got long c............................ hair.
4 He's got a b............................ and a m............................ and a rather c............................ face.
5 She's got long, s............................ hair and is t............................-faced.

7.2
15 marks
Answer the questions about words for describing people.

Example What is the opposite of long hair?   short hair

1 What is the adjective from *waves* used to describe hair?
2 Is *auburn* hair reddish-brown or blonde?
3 Is *stout* a synonym of *plump* or of *slim*?
4 Which sounds less unkind: calling someone *fat* or calling them *overweight*?
5 As you get older, do you get more or fewer *wrinkles*?
6 If someone is *anorexic*, what do they try to avoid doing?
7 If we say someone has a nice *figure*, are we referring to their face or their body?
8 If we say someone has a lovely *complexion*, are we referring to their face or their body?
9 If someone is *ginger-haired*, is their hair red or black?
10 If someone's hair is *receding*, do they have more or less hair than they used to?
11 If someone is *stocky*, are they broad and solid or tall and thin?
12 If you *sunbathe*, what do you probably hope to get?
13 If someone is *well-built*, are they muscular or plumpish?
14 If someone looks *twentyish*, how old are they likely to be?
15 Name three facial features.

7.3
10 marks
Write P (Positive) or N (Negative) beside each of these words.

Example skinny N

1 obese
2 elegant
3 slim
4 scruffy
5 stunning

6 messy
7 handsome
8 fat
9 smart
10 good-looking

Your score

/35

Describing people: character

8.1 **Match the synonyms.**

10 marks

Example half-witted – dim

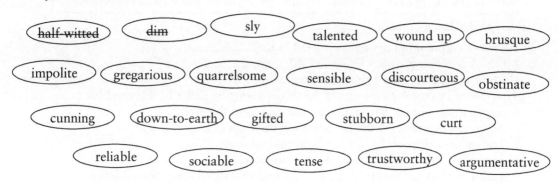

8.2 **Rewrite the sentences using the adjectives in the box.**

10 marks

brainless cruel easy-going extroverted eccentric envious
jealous nosy optimistic sensitive sincere

Example Jessica always sees the bright side of things. Jessica's optimistic.

1 Rob always wants what other people have got.
2 Suzie takes everything calmly and never gets upset.
3 Mickey seems to enjoy pulling the cat's tail really hard.
4 You know that Clare always means what she says.
5 Julia hates it when her boyfriend talks to another woman.
6 Becky only ever wears purple clothes and purple lipstick.
7 When we have visitors, our neighbour Bob is always at his window watching who it is.
8 Emma always gets upset if she feels she is being criticised or laughed at.
9 Ali is a very outgoing boy, always chatting and laughing with his friends.
10 Maggie can't do the simplest thing without making some silly mistake.

8.3 **Does the speaker approve / not approve of these people? Put A (approves) or**
DA (doesn't approve).

10 marks

Example Jack's miserly. DA

1 Sam is broad-minded.   5 Anna's naïve.   9 Dave's pig-headed.
2 Sarah is original.   6 Tanya is generous.   10 Debby's thrifty.
3 Mark's arrogant.   7 Joanna is assertive.
4 John is pushy.   8 Milly is abrupt.

8.4 **Complete these sentences by disagreeing with some of the opinions in 8.3. Use the**
adjectives from the box.

5 marks

determined economical extravagant tight-fisted unprincipled weird

Example I don't agree about Jack. I'd call him economical .

1 I don't agree about Sam. I'd call him ....
2 I don't agree about Sarah. I think she's just ....
3 I'm not sure about Tanya. I think she's too ....
4 I think you're being hard on Dave. I think he's just ....
5 You're being too kind to Debby. In my opinion, she's ....

Your score

/35

Idioms describing people

9.1 **Complete the sentences with the words from the box.**

10 marks

| ball   bones   ~~gold~~   good   heights   pain   pet   piece   place   sand   shoulders |

Example He has a heart of ....gold.......... .

1 There's no point in burying your head in the ....
2 I think our new boss is a bit of an odd-............................... .
3 Come on, get up. Don't be such a lazy-............................... .
4 He refused to climb to the top of the tower, saying he didn't have a head for ....
5 Sophie's nice but her flat-mate's a............................... in the neck.
6 Adam can be annoying but his heart's in the right ....
7 The children were as .... as gold all day.
8 The other children all say that Anna is the teacher's ....
9 Max's work is head and .... above that of all the other students.
10 I don't like my brother's new girlfriend. I think she's a nasty .... of work.

9.2 **Put P if the sentence is positive and N if it is negative.**

10 marks

Example Zara's got a heart of gold. P

1 Tessa's got a head like a sieve.
2 Izzy has her head screwed on.
3 I think Ben's gone round the bend.
4 Lee has a good head for figures.
5 You can rely on Tom to keep his head.
6 Victoria's as hard as nails.
7 Mark's an awkward customer.
8 Ahmet's usually top of the class.
9 Rita has her head in the clouds.
10 Leila's a bit of a big-head.

9.3 **Look at the sentences in 9.2. Which person ...**

10 marks

Example ... does particularly well at school? Ahmet

1 ... is very sensible?
2 ... has a high opinion of themselves?
3 ... remains calm in difficult situations?
4 ... forgets things easily?
5 ... seems unaware of the real world?
6 ... is very kind and generous?
7 ... is behaving in a crazy way?
8 ... is difficult to deal with?
9 ... has a talent for maths?
10 ... lacks sympathy for others?

9.4 **Underline the correct meanings of the expressions.**

5 marks

Example If you say someone *keeps their head*, are you talking about <u>how calm they are</u> or how intelligent they are?

1 If someone *gets on your nerves*, do they annoy you or inspire you?
2 If you call someone *a know-all*, do you admire their knowledge or feel irritated by it?
3 If you say your political position is *middle-of-the-road*, are you extreme or average in your views?
4 If you say a child is *as good as gold*, are you talking about their behaviour or their schoolwork?
5 If you say that what someone has done is *over the top*, are you admiring or criticising their behaviour?

Your score
/35

10.1 Read the statements and tick True or False.   True   False

10 marks

Example If you *fancy* someone, you find them unattractive.   ☐   ☑

1 If you *despise* someone, you don't like or respect them.   ☐   ☐
2 *Workmate* is less formal than *colleague*.   ☐   ☐
3 A *steady boyfriend / girlfriend* is just a casual relationship. ☐   ☐
4 To *adore* or *idolise* means to like very much indeed.   ☐   ☐
5 Your *parents-in-law* are your husband's or wife's parents.   ☐   ☐
6 Someone's *ex* is their future husband or wife.   ☐   ☐
7 If you *make it up with someone*, you are no longer friends.   ☐   ☐
8 If you don't *see eye to eye with someone*, your opinions differ. ☐   ☐
9 Your *contacts* are your closest friends.   ☐   ☐
10 A *housemate* is someone who lives next door.   ☐   ☐

10.2 Rewrite each sentence using the word (or word part) in brackets.

5 marks

Example Louise is no longer Pete's wife. (ex)
           Louise is Pete's ex.

1 I loathe my new boss. (stand)
2 She's had a lot of arguments with her colleagues. (fallen)
3 Jo and I have all our lessons together. (-mates)
4 I think Rick's in a relationship with his best friend's wife. (affair)
5 Bethany admires her older brother. (looks)

10.3 Complete the sentences with the correct words. (The first letters are given.)

15 marks

Example If you want to end a relationship with someone on a social network site,
           you un*friend* them.

1 I g.................... on well w.................... all my workmates and we have a lot of fun.
2 He's not really a friend, just a c.................... a.................... .
3 He doesn't just love her – he absolutely a.................... her.
4 If you a.................... someone as your friend on Facebook, you can then i....................
    with each other through the site.
5 Everyone else said they liked the film but it l.................... me cold.
6 We were told we could each bring our husband or wife or other p.................... to the
    office dinner.
7 I like writing a blog and most days I receive some very interesting c.................... on it.
8 We haven't had a proper chat for ages – I hope we can get t.................... soon.
9 We were b.................... friends for a while but then we f.................... out for some
    reason or other and now we hardly ever s.................... each other.
10 I wouldn't say we were in a s.................... relationship – we just go out together every
    now and then.

10.4 Choose the correct words in these sentences.

5 marks

Example Lizzy and I usually see eye *on / at / (to)* eye on such matters.

1 Although Paul loved the concert, it didn't *make / do / get* anything for me.
2 When I moved to another town, it took me a while to *make / have / get* friends
3 He says he's usually more attracted *for / to / with* tall, dark girls than short, fair ones.
4 She always makes me feel that she looks down *over / on / to* me.

Your score

/35   5 I get on very well with my *parents-in-law / parent-ins-law / parent-in-laws*.

11.1 Answer the questions.

10 marks

Example What kitchen implement is useful when you are preparing potatoes for a meal? *a peeler*

1 What kitchen implement is used for opening wine bottles?
2 What do you use for changing channels on the TV?
3 What do you need to use if your mobile's battery is low?
4 What do you put your clothes on when you iron them?
5 What do people use to avoid putting hot plates onto the dining table?
6 What do put jackets and dresses on in the wardrobe?
7 What do you plug electrical items into?
8 You drop a cup on the floor and it breaks. What do you use to sweep it up?
9 What do people usually cut up vegetables on?
10 What implement is used for cutting food like cheese into very small pieces?

11.2 Label the rooms / features of this house. (The first letters are given.)

13 marks

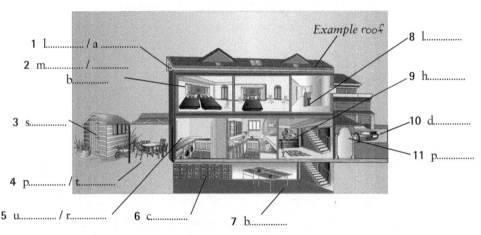

Example roof

1 l.............. / a ....
2 m.............. /
   b..............
3 s..............
4 p.............. / t..............
5 u.............. / r..............
6 c..............
7 b..............
8 l..............
9 h..............
10 d..............
11 p..............

11.3 Match the type of house with the correct definition.

7 marks

Example a flat that doesn't share facilities with another flat   [f]
1 a house with only one storey   [ ]
2 a large house with a big garden   [ ]
3 a house that is not joined to any other house   [ ]
4 a small house in the country or a village   [ ]
5 a house that is part of a row of other houses   [ ]
6 a small flat with one room for living and sleeping in [ ]
7 a house that is joined on one side to another house   [ ]

a a studio flat
b a cottage
c a semi
d a villa
e a bungalow
f a self-contained flat
g a terraced house
h a detached house

11.4 Complete the sentences with the words from the box.

5 marks

| loft conversion   shed   patio   studio   ~~study~~   drive |

Example Jack's a novelist and usually writes in a lovely book-lined ....*study*.......... at home.

1 It's lovely and warm outside – shall we have dinner on the ....?
2 We don't have a garage but the .... is big enough for two cars.
3 We've just had a .... creating an extra bedroom at the top of the house.
4 We keep all our garden tools in the .... at the bottom of the garden.
5 The artist has a large .... where the light is perfect for painting.

(Your score)

/35

12.1
10 marks

Choose the correct words in these sentences.

Example I wonder why the TV isn't *coming /(working)/ running*.

1 My computer has just *blocked / twisted / crashed*.
2 The little girl fell and *grazed / spilt / cracked* her knee.
3 The clock needs a new battery – it's *crushed / stopped / locked*.
4 Hari *dented / tripped / twisted* his ankle on the school skiing trip.
5 Watch you don't *dent / block / bang* your head on that low beam.
6 Granny's *crushed / mislaid / bruised* her glasses – can you help her look for them?
7 I'm afraid the car battery's *slow / flat / fast* and the car won't start.
8 I hope the tea I spilt won't leave a *stain / leak / flood* on your carpet.
9 Charlie *cracked / crashed / tripped* on a toy that was lying on the stairs.
10 The dishwasher *ran / broke / fell* down at the weekend.

12.2
20 marks

Match each problem with its possible cause. Then choose the correct word to complete each cause.

Example The door handle's come off. | h |

1 Sam's locked himself out. ☐
2 This bowl is chipped. ☐
3 The bucket's leaking. ☐
4 The lights aren't working. ☐
5 My car won't start. ☐
6 The sink's blocked. ☐
7 The kitchen floor is flooded. ☐
8 The window's been smashed. ☐
9 The biscuits are burnt. ☐
10 There's a stain on the carpet. ☐

a The oven must have been too *hot / cold*.
b Perhaps someone was trying to break *in / up*.
c The battery could be *full / flat*.
d Perhaps Jo threw *the coffee grounds / some hot water* in it.
e Pete *drank / spilt* some juice on it.
f Perhaps someone *mended / dropped* it.
g It must have *a bump / a hole* in it.
h A (screw)*/ tooth* had come loose.
i The washing machine must be *new / leaking*.
j He left his *keys / credit card* on the kitchen table.
k There must be a *power / short* cut.

12.3
5 marks

Match the sentences with the pictures.

Example It's burnt. | c |
1 It's chipped. ☐
2 It's dented. ☐
3 It's fallen off. ☐
4 It's crushed. ☐
5 It's cracked. ☐

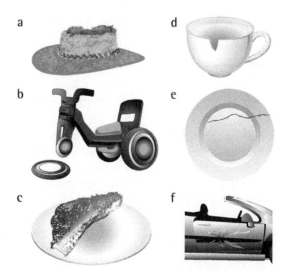

Your score
/35

13.1 Complete the sentences with the correct words. (The first letters are given.)

10 marks

Example The area has suffered............ several droughts recently.
1 Several buildings were d........................ in the bomb blast, but fortunately no one was
   i........................ .
2 After the battle the d........................ were buried and the w........................ were taken to a
   military hospital.
3 There was a serious famine and millions s........................ to death.
4 The volcano has not e........................ for a hundred years.
5 When the c........................ war began, many people fled across the border, ending up as
   r........................ in neighbouring countries.
6 There has been a report of a major a........................ on the motorway and it is feared that there
   have been a number of c........................ .

13.2 Put the letters in the correct order to make words connected with illness.

5 marks

Example PICEMIDE   an illness affecting large numbers of people *epidemic*

1 SIBERA   a disease that can be caught from the bite of an infected cat, dog or fox
2 AMALIRA   a disease that can be caught from a mosquito bite
3 SIDA   a disease affecting the immune system that has spread through the
                    world since the 1980s
4 HOLECAR, PITHODY two diseases that can be caught from infected food or water

13.3 Put the words from the box in the correct bubbles.

10 marks

casualty   drought   earthquake   flood   ~~hurricane~~   landslide
survivor   tornado   typhoon   victim   volcano

STRONG
WINDS

hurricane

LAND
MOVEMENT

WET / DRY

PEOPLE

13.4 Complete the sentences with the words from the box.

10 marks

broke   damaged   erupted   injured   ~~resulted~~   shook
spread   starved   suffered   swept   wounded

Example The explosion ....*resulted*.......... in a number of casualties.

1 An earthquake .... the city centre at 6.40 this morning.
2 The flu epidemic .... more rapidly than expected.
3 War .... out because of a border disagreement.
4 A hurricane .... across the island, destroying many houses.
5 The floods .... many homes and farms.
6 A number of people were .... when the volcano ....
7 Many people .... to death in last year's famine.
8 The region has .... terribly from drought over the last few years.
9 After the battle there were many dead and .... on both sides.

Your score

/35

14.1 Read the statements and tick True or False.

10 marks

	True	False
Example A public school in the UK is actually a private school.	✓	☐
1 *To pass an exam* means the same as *to sit an exam*.	☐	☐
2 There are usually more students in a seminar than there are in a tutorial.	☐	☐
3 A master's degree is usually a post-graduate degree.	☐	☐
4 A comprehensive school is only for the cleverest pupils.	☐	☐
5 A crèche is for the oldest pupils at school.	☐	☐
6 A project can be a kind of extended homework.	☐	☐
7 A college is usually more academic than a university.	☐	☐
8 Students go to lectures to listen to a lecturer.	☐	☐
9 A workshop is a class teaching students business skills.	☐	☐
10 The word *field* can be used to mean *area of study*.	☐	☐

14.2 Match words from the bubble on the left with words from the bubble on the right to form compound nouns.

7 marks

Example further education

Left bubble:
further
continuous
teacher-training
blended
graduation
school-leaving
primary
post-graduate

Right bubble:
college
degree
ceremony
education
school
learning
assessment
age

14.3 Complete the sentences with the correct words. (The first letters are given.)

10 marks

Example I failed my exam first time round so I'm going to r_esit_ it next month.
1 If you s............................... classes, you're bound to d............... badly in your exam.
2 Did you p............................... your geography exam?
3 I got a very good m............................... for my last essay.
4 My brother is doing a PhD and he's writing a t............................... on animal behaviour.
5 Most university students do their first d............................... in three or four years.
6 It is not easy to gain a............................... to a top university.
7 We usually have to s............................... our homework assignments online.
8 C............................... education here starts at the age of five.
9 Very few students in this country are lucky enough to receive a g............................... to finance their studies.

14.4 Choose the correct words in these sentences.

8 marks

Example Rob wants to be a primary school *professor / lecturer / teacher*.

1 The LMS our college uses makes it easy for tutors to *teach / monitor / submit* students' work.
2 I'm planning to do a *grant / grade / module* on romantic poetry next term.
3 If Dev had done more work, he wouldn't have *skipped / failed / passed* his exams.
4 At the end of my course I had to write a ten-thousand-word *dissertation / mark / diploma*.
5 Bethany has made very good *projects / tutorials / progress* with her French this year.
6 As soon as I *pass / graduate / submit* from university, I'll start looking for a job.
7 When children finish primary school, they move into *further / higher / secondary* education.
8 You have to pass an exam to get into a *grammar / comprehensive / nursery* school.

Your score
/35

15.1 **Correct the mistakes in these sentences.**
10 marks

Example It's getting harder ~~to do~~ a living as a musician. *to make*

1 What does your sister do to a living?
2 The union is encouraging its members to go in strike.
3 Orla is in flexi-time so she usually gets to work at 7 and leaves at 3.
4 My sister has got a new job as a publicity relations officer.
5 I go to job by bike most days.
6 When the company was taken over several staff were laid out.
7 Maria expects to be promoted to a new work soon.
8 The interests of the staff are defended by two unions representatives.
9 Will you take the job if you are offering it?
10 A child-minder looks for other people's children in her own home.

15.2 **Put the words from the box in the correct columns.**
10 marks

banker carpenter diplomat economist electrician firefighter judge physiotherapist plumber receptionist scientist

professions	trades
banker	

15.3 **Match the words on the left with the words on the right to form collocations.**
10 marks

Example get	d	a publishing
1 be made		b on strike
2 work		c shiftwork
3 take		d the sack
4 be in		e extra responsibility
5 make		f paternity leave
6 do		g redundant
7 go		h early retirement
8 apply		i a living
9 take on		j for a job
10 be on		k nine-to-five

15.4 **Which word / phrase is being defined?**
5 marks

Example time off work because of illness *sick leave*

1 a person who loves work too much ....
2 time that a mother takes off work when her baby is born ....
3 a person who works for a government department ....
4 a person who does a job that requires no training or qualifications ....
5 a member of a company's board ....

Your score
/35

16.1
10 marks

Match words from the bubble on the left with words from the bubble on the right to form collocations.

Example to get feedback

Left bubble:
~~to get~~
to launch
worth
customer
to make
market
to do
a business
stiff
order
to build

Right bubble:
plan
care
research
books
competition
contacts
business
~~feedback~~
a new range
a profit
the risk

16.2
10 marks

Match words / expressions from the box with the definitions.

> corporation custom-built expand feedback ~~firm~~ manufacture
> potential priority put forward recession roll out

Example company ....*firm*........

1 produce goods in large numbers, usually in a factory ....
2 something so important it will be dealt with first ....
3 propose, suggest ....
4 make bigger ....
5 possible ....
6 specially made for a particular customer or purpose ....
7 large company or group of companies ....
8 make available for the first time ....
9 information about what people think of a product or service ....
10 period of low economic activity ....

16.3
10 marks

Choose the correct words in these sentences.

Example There is *big /* (*stiff*) */ hard* competition in this line of business.

1 Going *forward / through / out*, we plan to start exporting to China.
2 We've been finding it difficult to *achieve / realise / access* new markets.
3 I hope our new range will *buy / sell / pay* well.
4 CEO stands for Chief *Executing / Execution / Executive* Officer.
5 We plan to *expand / launch / put forward* our new sports car in May.
6 When do you think we should roll *off / out / over* our new series of computer games?
7 All our kitchens are *custom- / customer- / customs-* built to suit your needs.
8 Building *plans / profits / contacts* is an important aspect of any business's strategy.
9 The company's order *books / papers / forms* are full until the end of the year.
10 Do you think that investing in that firm is worth *risk / the risk / to risk*?

16.4
5 marks

Complete the sentences with: *a profit, profits, business* or *businesses*.

Example Nicky has always dreamt of starting ...*a business*.... of her own.

1 It was several years before the company was able to make ....
2 The government's new policy aims to help small ....
3 The firm saw a steady rise in .... last year.
4 We did a lot more .... in Australia this year.
5 The company's .... have remained strong for many years.

(Your score)
/35

17.1 **Label the sports.**

10 marks

Example ....golf.... 3 .... 6 .... 9 ....

1 .... 4 .... 7 .... 10 ....

2 .... 5 .... 8 ....

17.2 **What do you call the people who do these sports?**

10 marks

Example long-distance running – *a long-distance runner*

1 tennis ....
2 canoeing ....
3 gymnastics ....
4 archery ....
5 sprinting ....

6 mountaineering ....
7 horse-racing ....
8 football ....
9 squash ....
10 swimming ....

17.3 **Complete the sentences with the words from the box.**

10 marks

| final ~~held~~ knocked make qualified referee round set spectator sports trophy |

Example Mark ....held.......... the school's high-jump record for a couple of years.

1 The person who takes decisions about penalties and so on in a football match is the

....
2 Azeem is hoping to .... a new record for the men's 100 metres this afternoon.
3 Do you think your team will .... it to the finals?
4 The town has some excellent .... facilities.
5 The team will display the .... in a special cabinet in their club house.
6 Irish supporters are delighted that their team has .... for the World Cup.
7 Jack played very well but unfortunately got .... out in the second ....
8 Do you prefer playing football or being a .... ?
9 I was very pleased to reach the semi-.............................. .

17.4 **What do you hold in your hand when you are ...**

5 marks

Example ... playing golf? *a club*

1 ... playing baseball? ....
2 ... playing hockey? ....
3 ... playing table tennis? ....
4 ... rowing? ....
5 ... playing snooker? ....

Your score

/35

18.1 Put the letters in the correct order to make words, then put the words in the correct columns.

10 marks

Example TABLEL *ballet*

1 ROTYPE
2 SCARECIM
3 CENDA
4 SLOVEN

5 PLUSCRETU
6 HATTERE
7 TRECUCATHIER

8 PARIBOGESHI
9 TINNIPAG
10 AREPO

literature	fine art	performing art
		ballet

18.2 Choose the correct words in these sentences.

10 marks

Example An architect's job is to *produce / draw / (design)* buildings.

1 I love watching a potter *turn / throw / fold* a pot.
2 This evening writers are reading *extracts / copies / reviews* from their own books.
3 James Herriot wrote a great *passage / work / series* of books about the life of a vet.
4 I love reading novels with a historical *setting / character / passage*.
5 A *still life / portrait / landscape* is a painting of a person.
6 You can see some wonderful works of *art / arts / artists* in this gallery.
7 An *original / abstract / artistic* painting shows shapes and colours rather than people or places that can be recognised.
8 The *critiques / criticisms / critics* have written in a very positive way about the play.
9 That writer always constructs a clever and interesting *bestseller / plot / publication*.
10 More and more *reproductions / novelists / e-books* are being downloaded these days.

18.3 Complete the sentences with the words from the box.

6 marks

art lovers   arts and crafts   ~~the arts pages~~   fine arts   art   arts   works of art

Example I always read ....*the arts pages*........ in the Sunday paper first.

1 Rich people often choose to use some of their wealth to buy ....
2 Tickets to the exhibition would make an excellent present for any.. among your friends and family.
3 The .... include music and drama as well as painting and sculpture.
4 The college is running an evening course on the .... of novel writing.
5 Traditional local .... include beautiful silver jewellery, colourful knitted sweaters and some very unusual wood carvings.
6 If someone is studying a .... course at our college, they can choose to specialise in either sculpture, painting or ceramics in their third year.

18.4 Which words are being defined? (The first letters are given.)

9 marks

Example painting produced by an artist (not a copy) o r i g i n a l

1 copy of a painting   r _ _ _ _ _ _ _ _ _ _
2 person who creates statues   s _ _ _ _ _ _ _
3 what a critic writes   r _ _ _ _ _
4 adjective describing a serious writer   l _ _ _ _ _ _ _
5 person in a novel or film   c _ _ _ _ _ _ _ _
6 extract from a novel or story   p _ _ _ _ _ _
7 adjective describing a person who is good at art a _ _ _ _ _ _ _
8 very popular and successful book   b _ _ _ _ _ _ _ _ _
9 person who designs buildings   a _ _ _ _ _ _ _ _

Your score
/35

19.1 Choose the correct words in this review.

10 marks

> There is an interesting new *performance* /(*production*) of the musical *Chess* on at the Apollo Theatre this week.
> The [1] *cast / script* is excellent, demonstrating first-class acting as well as singing skills. The large [2] *scene / stage* which this new [3] *place / venue* offers, is well-used, with striking black and white [4] *sets / backgrounds*, making the show a powerful visual experience. The [5] *costumes / dresses* were absolutely right for the1960s, the period in which the story is [6] *set / placed*. Some of the original [7] *conversation / dialogue* has been adapted to include contemporary references but this has been done with great skill. I have nothing but praise for the skilled [8] *direction / promotion* of the show and the [9] *viewers / audience* were as appreciative as I was, giving the performers a standing ovation at the end of the evening. I am sure that this will not be the only rave [10] *critic / review* in the papers this week.

19.2 Match the words with their definitions.

10 marks

Example clothes worn by actors | d | a appear
1 the words of a play or film | | b scene
2 a person who entertains by telling jokes | | c director
3 publicise | | d costumes
4 be (in a show) | | e score
5 someone watching a TV show | | f promote
6 section of a play or film | | g audience
7 person in charge of a play or film | | h script
8 people watching a performance in a theatre | | i viewer
9 place on which actors perform | | j stage
10 music used in a film | | k comedian

19.3 Match the beginning of each sentence with its ending.

10 marks

Example The score of the film was written | g | a the ballet or the opera.
1 James Roe gives a wonderful | | b in nineteenth-century Rome.
2 The film succeeds in capturing | | c performance in the play.
3 I don't mind whether we go to | | d entertainers I've ever seen.
4 Do you know what's | | e modern dance.
5 The cinema's showing | | f the atmosphere of the time.
6 Who wrote the screenplay | | g by a well-known composer.
7 The play is set | | h Bollywood films all week.
8 That comedian's one of the best | | i production of *Cats*.
9 I'm reading a great book about | | j on at the cinema today?
10 I enjoyed the school | | k for the film?

19.4 Are these sentences correct or incorrect? Add *the* if necessary.

5 marks

Example We went to ballet when we were in St Petersburg.
        Incorrect. We went to *the* ballet when we were in St Petersburg.

1 I love watching modern dance.
2 Katie is very enthusiastic about theatre.
3 Do come to cinema with us this evening!
(Your score) 4 What made you so interested in ballet?
/35 5 My parents took me to opera on Saturday.

20.1 **Correct the mistakes in these sentences.**

10 marks

Example Olaf is a very good ~~drumer~~. *drummer*

1 My tastes of music are very different from my parents'.
2 I loved the musics they played at the concert, didn't you?
3 Nathan is a very talented base guitarist.
4 Helena can't read music but she's very good at playing on ear.
5 Marek only needs to hear a tune once to be able to pick it off on the piano.
6 Which do you prefer – pop or classic music?
7 What do you think of the leader singer in the band?
8 I'm not really onto folk music.
9 Every culture has its own traditional ways of doing music.
10 An album is made up of a number of individual tricks.

20.2 **Put the letters in the correct order to make different types of music.**

5 marks

Example KOLF ....*folk*............

1 PIPHOH ....
2 ZAJZ ....
3 SALLISCAC ....
4 BRAND ....
5 PAR ....

20.3 **Complete the sentences with the words from the box.**

10 marks

become canned composed has ~~rap~~ read stream sync taste trained tune

Example Jody is a successful ....*rap*............ artist.

1 Why do so many hotels insist on playing .... music in their lifts?
2 I need to .... my new MP3 player with my computer.
3 We were able to .... the concert and watch it on our computer at the same time as it was happening in Sydney.
4 All the members of that family are .... musicians.
5 One of the first things you do in music lessons is learn how to .... music.
6 I can't play the piano well but I can pick out a ....
7 The band .... most of their songs themselves.
8 Lara .... a very good ear for music. I quite envy her.
9 Bel's dream is to .... a keyboard player in a band.
10 Henrik's father doesn't approve of his .... in music.

20.4 **Are these definitions correct or incorrect? If they are wrong, correct them.**

10 marks

Example guitarist – a type of musical instrument *Incorrect – a type of musician*

1 a drum – an instrument that you play by hitting it with your hand or a stick
2 a bass guitar – a guitar that plays the highest range of notes
3 60s music – music for older people
4 a playlist – a list of music you can choose to download from an online shop
5 talented – gifted
6 a keyboard – a type of musician
7 sync – short for *syncopate*
8 a soundtrack – music from an album
9 r and b – short for rhythm and blues
10 into – enthusiastic about

Your score

/35

21.1 What is the same and what is different about these pairs?

10 marks

Example *a starter* and *a dessert*
same = both are courses in a meal;
different = a starter comes **before** the main course, a dessert comes **after** it

1 *set menu* and *à la carte*
2 *unripe* and *underdone*
3 *hot* and *mild*
4 *cutlery* and *napkins*
5 a *vegetarian* and a *non-meat-eater*

21.2 Match the words with the correct examples / definitions.

10 marks

Example sweet ☐ d

1	bitter	☐	a with little flavour
2	sour	☐	b pleasant, slightly salty or with herbs
3	bland	☐	c with too much sugar
4	sickly	☐	d e.g. a perfectly ripe strawberry
5	savoury	☐	e with no flavour at all
6	spicy	☐	f heavy and hard to digest
7	tasteless	☐	g you don't want to stop eating it
8	stodgy	☐	h sharp, unpleasant
9	overdone	☐	i e.g. a curry
10	moreish	☐	j sharp, e.g. fruit that is not ripe
			k cooked for too long

21.3 Write P (positive) or N (negative) next to each statement.

6 marks

Example These potatoes are undercooked.   N

1 The pudding was a little heavy.
2 The milk has gone off.
3 The stew was very tasty.
4 Sadie always serves a balanced meal
5 These crisps are very moreish.
6 Joe eats a lot of junk food.

21.4 Choose the correct words in these sentences.

9 marks

Example I prefer a (mild)/ *spicy* curry to a hot one.

1 Now, children, would you like some ice cream for *seconds / afters*?
2 *Organic / Processed* food is better for you but it tends to be more expensive.
3 We had to *make / cancel* our booking at the restaurant because Grandma was ill.
4 Please do *help / give* yourselves to some more salad.
5 Let me *refill / repour* your glass – just say *when / where*.
6 Would you like any side *plates / dishes* with your main course?
7 This restaurant always has good *puddings / specials* – whatever fish has just been caught.
8 There is some delicious asparagus in *time / season* at the moment.

Your score

/35

22.1
Which words are being defined? (The first letters are given.)

Example a very large sea, e.g. the Pacific   o*cean*...............

  1 an area of flat land   p...............
  2 a hole that sends out hot water and steam   g...............
  3 a river of ice   g...............
  4 land with sea on three sides   p...............
  5 a valley with very steep sides   g...............
  6 where a river meets the sea   m...............
  7 the top of a mountain   s...............
  8 a river that flows into another river   t...............
  9 where a river starts   s...............
10 a small river   s...............

22.2
Do these places need *the* in front of them? Put *the* or – .

Example ...*the*.... Pacific

  1 .... Himalayas
  2 .... Russia
  3 .... United States
  4 .... Lake Baikal
  5 .... Amazon
  6 .... Australia
  7 .... Mount Kilimanjaro
  8 .... West Indies
  9 .... Caribbean
10 .... Straits of Gibraltar

22.3
Put the words from the box in the correct bubbles.

~~bay~~ waterfall coast delta foot gulf peak estuary shore ridge cliff

Where land meets sea   (*bay*)

Part of mountain   ( )

Part of river   ( )

22.4
Match the collocations.

Example *barren plains*

adjectives	nouns
~~barren~~	crops
thermal	fields
ice	~~plains~~
active	population
the country's ageing	volcano
the area's most profitable	springs

23.1 Put the jumbled letters in the correct order.

10 marks

Example STEWA disposal ......*waste disposal*......

1 greenhouse FEFTCE ....
2 BARONC footprint ....
3 SILFOS fuels ....
4 BALLOG warming ....
5 METALIC change ....
6 CIDA rain ....
7 ROPLA ice cap ....
8 GAEDENERDN species ....
9 air NILTOPULO ....
10 NOOZE depletion ....

23.2 Complete the table.

16 marks

noun	verb	adjective	adverb
destruction	destroy	(1)	(2) ....
(3)	dispose	(4)	
environment, (5)		(6)	(7) ....
globalisation	(8)	(9)	(10) ....
(11) .... , (12)	pollute	(13)	
danger	(14)	(15)	
ecology		(16)	

23.3 Explain what the underlined words mean.

9 marks

Example This part of the country is <u>over-populated</u>, with the result that there is too much pressure on the infrastructure.
　　　　too many people live there

1 The city suffers much less from <u>smog</u> than it used to.
2 There are at least 15,000 <u>species</u> of butterfly in the world.
3 We visited an amazing nature <u>reserve</u> when we were in South Africa.
4 Herring used to be plentiful in the waters off our shores but <u>over-fishing</u> in the past means they are now quite scarce.
5 There are a number of different theories as to why dinosaurs became <u>extinct</u>.
6 Many businesses now are increasingly aware of <u>green</u> issues.
7 <u>Disposable</u> nappies are convenient for parents but not so good for the environment.
8 It is much easier to <u>recycle</u> glass, cardboard or paper than, say, plastics.
9 Conservation organisations <u>worldwide</u> are doing all they can to help endangered animals and plants.

Your score
/35

24.1
10 marks

Complete the places.

Example housing ....*estate*...............

1 swimming ....
2 art ....
3 opera ....
4 radio ....
5 registry ....
6 department ....
7 law ....
8 taxi ....
9 skating ....
10 golf ....

24.2
10 marks

Which is the odd one out? Explain why.

Example bus service, car hire, (football pitch), parking meter
         'Football pitch' is connected with sport; the others are connected with transport.

1 youth hostel, police station, B and B, hotel
2 citizens' advice bureau, job centre, garden centre, health centre
3 suburbs, vandalism, overcrowding, traffic jams
4 picturesque, filthy, elegant, spacious
5 theatre, concert hall, museum, chemist's

24.3
9 marks

Complete the text with the correct forms of the words in capitals.

Aberdeen is a ....*bustling*........ city in the north-east of Scotland with   BUSTLE
a ⁽¹⁾ .... of over 250,000. It is on the coast and has a beautiful   POPULATE
beach and an excellent harbour. It is one of the ⁽²⁾ .... cities   LIVELY
in Scotland with plenty of nightlife. It is also a ⁽³⁾ .... centre with   CULTURE
an art gallery showing work by both traditional and more ⁽⁴⁾ ....   ADVENTURE
artists. The city has two ⁽⁵⁾ .... centres, one at the mouth of the   HISTORY
River Dee and the other at the mouth of the River Don. The ⁽⁶⁾ ....   RESIDE
areas of the city are mainly in the outskirts. The centre is ⁽⁷⁾ ....   SPACE
with broad streets and imposing granite public ⁽⁸⁾ .... It is a   BUILD
wealthy city with few of the problems such as ⁽⁹⁾ .... that affect   VANDAL
many other modern urban areas.

24.4
6 marks

Match each place with what happens there.

Example car park [f]
1 library   □
2 Town Hall   □
3 take-away   □
4 estate agent's   □
5 slum   □
6 industrial estate   □

a where people find a place to live
b where lots of small businesses are based
c where people live in poor, overcrowded houses
d where you borrow books
e where you buy prepared food to eat at home
f where people leave vehicles
g where local government meetings are held

Your score

/35

25.1 Label the pictures with the words from the box.

10 marks

| bat beak bud branch frog hoof ~~mane~~ nest snail trunk worm |

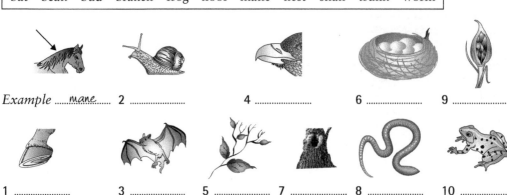

Example .....mane...... 2 .... 4 .... 6 .... 9 ....

1 .... 3 .... 5 .... 7 .... 8 .... 10 ....

25.2 Write the correct words. (The first letters are given.)

10 marks

Example Where do baby birds come from? e g g s

1 What do bees transfer from one flower to another? p _ _ _ _ _
2 Which bird can open out its tail in a beautiful fan of feathers? p _ _ _ _ _ _
3 What do you call the part of a plant that is underground? r _ _ _ _
4 What is the correct word for a cat's or dog's feet? p _ _ _
5 What does a bird have that allow it to fly? w _ _ _ _
6 What do you call the outer 'skin' of a tree? b _ _ _
7 Birds have feathers, but what do cats, for example, have? f _ _
8 What is a dangerous sea creature with lots of very sharp teeth? s _ _ _ _
9 What are the pretty coloured parts of a flower called? p _ _ _ _ _
10 What does a monkey have that a person doesn't? t _ _ _

25.3 Complete the sentences with the words from the box.

6 marks

Example Every autumn we ....collect.......... mushrooms in the forest.

1 Rabbits .... very rapidly.
2 I helped the man .... some apples he'd dropped.
3 What do you .... in your garden?
4 Our hens .... eggs almost every day.
5 Cherry trees are very beautiful when they .... in spring.
6 Please go and .... one or two nice roses to put in that vase.

| blossom |
| breed |
| ~~collect~~ |
| grow |
| lay |
| pick |
| pick up |

25.4 Choose the correct words in these sentences.

9 marks

Example Meat from a *shark / (deer) / frog* is called venison.

1 Find some nice dry *pollen / buds / twigs* and we'll try to start a bonfire.
2 The cat has ruined that chair with its sharp *claws / wings / fur*.
3 My grandfather used to *grow / pick / breed* horses.
4 The *whale / crab / seal* is the largest creature in the sea.
5 A *fox / frog / pigeon* is a kind of bird.
6 A *bark / bough / leaf* is a large branch of a tree.
7 Even people who don't know much about birds can recognise *worms / foxes / owls*.
8 A cat's *feathers / thorns / whiskers* are very sensitive and help it find its way around.
9 The man trained his horse to stamp its *horn / hoof / mane* once for yes and twice for no.

Your score

/35

26.1 Label the pictures with the words from the box.

10 marks

| belt | cuff | cardigan | coat | collar | helmet | buckle | pyjamas | sleeve | slippers | zip |

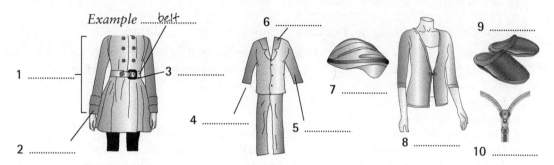

Example ....belt.......

1 ....
2 ....
3 ....
4 ....
5 ....
6 ....
7 ....
8 ....
9 ....
10 ....

26.2 Complete the text with the correct prepositions.

10 marks

I went shopping for clothes yesterday and tried ....on........ lots of different things. I've grown (1) .... (2) .... my old winter coat so I need a new one. First I tried one that I liked but it was too long and needed taking (3) .... It was also a bit tight and needed letting (4) .... as well. So then I tried one in a different style but that was too short and too loose so it needed letting (5) .... and taking (6) .... So I decided not to get a coat. I saw a lovely party dress and decided to try that (7) .... instead. I love changing (8) .... (9) .... my everyday clothes and dressing (10) .... for parties. The dress fitted me perfectly and so I bought it.

26.3 Match the pictures with the correct descriptions.

5 marks

Example a long-sleeved dress c

1 a plain shirt
2 a checked shirt
3 a tartan skirt
4 a flowery blouse
5 a striped top

a  b  c

d e  f

26.4 Choose the correct words in these sentences.

10 marks

Example A: Do those shoes *fit* / *match* you? B: No, they're too small.

1 Rosie, you've got your T-shirt on *outside in* / *inside out*!
2 That dress really *matches* / *suits* you, Tamara – it looks wonderful with your blond hair.
3 I wish I could look as *elegant* / *baggy* as Gina always does.
4 At the parade on Independence Day everyone dresses up in *designer* / *national* costume.
5 It isn't a formal party – the invitation says we should dress *elegantly* / *casually*.
6 I'd love to go to a romantic ball where everyone has to wear a *mask* / *helmet*.
7 I don't know how Ellie can wear shoes with such high *buttons* / *heels*.
8 In the story the princess puts on the clothes of a poor servant as a *disguise* / *costume* and goes out into the town without anyone recognising her.
9 All the children who passed the test were given a *sole* / *badge* to sew on their shirt.
10 I need to buy a new pair of *hoods* / *laces* for my walking boots.

Health and medicine

27.1
10 marks
Complete the sentences with the words from the box.

bandage temperature bruises indigestion injection
lump operation breathless ~~sore~~ pain virus

Example I think I'm getting flu. I've got a dreadful ....*sore*......... throat.

1 If your .... rises to 38°, take some paracetamol to bring it down.
2 Mike is having a small .... today; they're taking his wisdom teeth out.
3 We'll ask the nurse to put a .... on your ankle.
4 Jack was covered in .... after the rugby match.
5 Don't eat so fast – you'll get ....
6 The doctor says I've got some .... that's going round.
7 Daisy is quite unfit – she gets .... walking up one flight of stairs.
8 Tim hit his head on a shelf – that's why he's got a .... on his forehead.
9 I had to stop running because I had a .... in my side.
10 Have you recently had a tetanus .... ?

27.2
10 marks
Match the beginning of each sentence with its ending.

Example Ollie's leg will be | *b* |

1 Tom had to have an operation
2 Muneera's grandpa died
3 It took me several weeks to recover
4 When she was in the USA, Harriet picked
5 Even when he was ill, Sam didn't lose
6 On her first day skiing Ana sprained
7 It can take ten days or so to get
8 Take a teaspoonful
9 I've eaten so much cake that I feel
10 Heavy smokers are more likely to suffer

a up a nasty bug.
b in plaster for six weeks.
c on his leg.
d her ankle.
e of this medicine at 9 pm.
f a heart attack.
g of a stroke last year.
h quite sick.
i his appetite.
j over a bad cold.
k from the shock.

27.3
10 marks
Write the correct words. (The first letters are given.)

Example What word often completes this phrase – sickness and d *i a r r h o e a* ?

1 If you can't speak, what have you lost?   your v _ _ _ _
2 What verb means *to force a bone out of its correct position*?   d _ _ _ _ _ _ _ _
3 What is a more formal word for *a bug* (in the illness sense)?   i _ _ _ _ _ _ _ _
4 What adjective means *extremely tired*?   e _ _ _ _ _ _ _ _
5 What verb can be used in formal contexts to mean *catch or become ill with (a disease)*?   c _ _ _ _ _ _ _
6 How does your skin feel if you've been bitten by a mosquito?   it i _ _ _ _ _
7 What do your hands sometimes do if you feel nervous or afraid?   t _ _ _ _ _ _
8 How do you feel if your head is spinning?   d _ _ _ _
9 If an illness gives you spots, what is another word for those spots?   a r _ _ _
10 What verb means *to shake because you are cold*?   s _ _ _ _ _

27.4
5 marks
Combine words from the box to make compound nouns.

Example sunburn

Your score
/35

~~burn~~ blood throat ear eye pains
pressure sore ~~sun~~ chest ache black

Medicine and technology

28.1
10 marks

Complete the text with the words from the box. (You may need to change the form.)

> correct   describe   diagnose   connect   ~~make~~   manufacture
> operate   provide   treat   wear   use

Rapid advances in medical technology have been ....*made*.......... over the last few decades. For example, companies have (1) .... instruments that allow doctors to work at a distance from their patients. Patients can, for instance, (2) .... their symptoms to a doctor using Skype and then use instruments (3) .... to their computer to (4) .... the doctor with information about, say, their blood pressure or temperature. This enables the doctor to (5) .... their condition and decide how best to (6) .... it. Surgeons can even (7) .... on patients at a distance. A surgeon in South America can, for example (8) .... laser technology to (9) .... the eyesight of a patient in Europe so that they no longer need to (10) .... contact lenses or spectacles.

28.2
6 marks

Complete the sentences that describe the pictures.

Example The nurse is putting a .....*thermometer*..... in her mouth.

1 The man is walking on ....
2 The doctor is looking at an ....
3 The girl is putting in her ....
4 The man is sitting in a ....
5 The staff are using a .... to check the patient.
6 The man is wearing a ....

28.3
19 marks

Complete the sentences with the correct words. (The first letters are given.)

Example The disease can be cured if it is caught at an early s_t_ _a_ _g_ _e_ .

1 You don't need to have a g _ _ _ _ _ _ anaesthetic for this o _ _ _ _ _ _ _ _ , just a local one.
2 Glasses, also known as s _ _ _ _ _ _ _ _ _ , are used to correct people's v _ _ _ _ _ .
3 A p _ _ _ _ _ _ _ _ is a very effective d _ _ _ _ _ which surgeons can insert into the heart of a person with cardiac problems.
4 K _ _ _ _ _ _ surgery generally requires less recovery time than big operations.
5 My aunt was having a lot of pain walking until she received an a _ _ _ _ _ _ _ _ hip last year.
6 A v _ _ _ range of medical devices are available these days to help people with, for example, hearing d _ _ _ _ _ _ _ _ _ _ or mobility problems.
7 International d _ _ _ _ _ _ _ _ provide enormous banks of medical information and so have become an invaluable t _ _ _ for medical researchers.
8 Rapid a _ _ _ _ _ _ _ in medical technology in the last d _ _ _ _ _ mean that things are possible now that were inconceivable only ten years ago.
9 The staff at the hospital are h _ _ _ _ _ efficient.
10 I've worn contact l _ _ _ _ _ since I was a teenager; now I also need a hearing a _ _ .
11 When I was pregnant I measured my blood p _ _ _ _ _ _ _ at home and the machine sent the readings a _ _ _ _ _ _ _ _ _ _ _ _ to the doctor.

Your score
/35

29.1

10 marks

Choose the correct words in these sentences.

Example It's not a good idea to have too many *oily /* (*fizzy*) drinks.

1 Alcohol can be *harmful / harmless* especially when consumed in large quantities.
2 Eating more apples is one way of *raising / lowering* your cholesterol level.
3 There has been a *sharp / stiff* rise in the number of adults with a weight problem.
4 It's better for you to eat more fresh food than *processed / produced* food.
5 Eating plenty of vitamins helps to *increase / boost* your *immune / immunity* system.
6 Children who take too little *sport / exercise* risk becoming obese.
7 Spinach is a good *resource / source* of vitamin A.
8 Blueberries are said to improve *short-run / short-term* memory and slow the ageing *process / procedure*.

29.2

12 marks

Read the statements and tick True or False.

	True	False
Example Mental health refers to the health of the body.	☐	☑
1 *To maintain your fitness* means *to improve your fitness.*	☐	☐
2 *To reduce the risk of heart disease* means *to make heart disease less likely.*	☐	☐
3 *Wholemeal bread* is bread made from a range of different types of flour.	☐	☐
4 A *major* problem is an *insignificant* problem.	☐	☐
5 Depression is an illness where a person is unhappy and anxious for a long time.	☐	☐
6 A label showing the salt content of a food states how much salt there ought to be in it.	☐	☐
7 The noun from *obese* is *obesity.*	☐	☐
8 We say that bad habits like smoking *make harm to the body.*	☐	☐
9 Superfoods are foods that taste particularly good.	☐	☐
10 If you are *under stress* at work, it means that things are going smoothly.	☐	☐
11 *Exercise* can be both a noun and a verb.	☐	☐
12 *Fit* is an adjective meaning *unhealthy.*	☐	☐

29.3

8 marks

Correct the false sentences in 29.2.

Example Mental health refers to the health of the mind.

29.4

5 marks

Complete the sentences with: *food, foods, fruit* or *fruits.*

Example I eat at least five pieces of ......fruit...... every day.

1 Oranges, lemons, limes and grapefruit are all citrus ....
2 Raspberries are probably my favourite ....
3 The website lists many different ...., all with special medicinal properties.
4 Try not to eat so much .... with a high fat content.
5 Avoid fatty .... such as cheese, cream and butter.

Your score

/35

30.1 Which is the odd one out? Explain why.

10 marks

Example bus, lorry, car, (jumbo jet) *A bus, lorry or car travels on roads; a jumbo jet flies.*

1 cockpit, wings, platform, aisle
2 ticket collector, steward, deck, captain
3 terminal, breakdown service, port, petrol station
4 motorist, air traffic controller, ground staff, cabin crew
5 high speed train, buffet, ferry, express

30.2 Find the names of these things in the word square.

8 marks

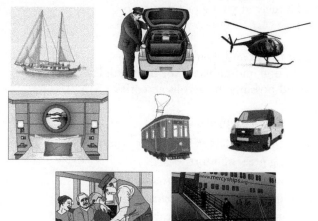

Z	H	B	T	E	R	T	C	I	L
V	E	L	R	A	D	U	K	O	I
S	L	V	A	N	X	Y	P	L	M
H	I	O	M	R	O	A	Y	I	N
I	C	O	N	D	U	C	T	O	R
B	O	O	T	V	C	H	L	O	P
M	P	U	N	C	A	T	N	U	R
A	T	E	S	X	B	Y	T	U	K
W	E	X	H	A	I	H	G	I	M
E	R	Q	G	A	N	G	W	A	Y
T	C	H	A	U	F	F	E	U	R

30.3 Which word / phrase matches these definitions?

12 marks

Example a corridor in a plane *an aisle*

1 a synonym for *held up*, e.g. *my flight was held up by fog* ....
2 uncomfortable feeling after flying across several time zones ....
3 illness that some people suffer from on a boat or ship ....
4 a long journey by sea ....
5 the long strip of tarmac where an aeroplane lands ....
6 a place where you can buy things without paying tax when you're travelling ....
7 describes a flight or landing that is not smooth (begins with *b*) ....
8 to wait for a seat to come available on a plane ....
9 a holiday on a boat visiting different places as you travel around ....
10 a booking for a particular place on, for example, a train ....
11 a phrasal verb meaning *to give someone a bed for the night* ....
12 a phrase with the word *time* that means *punctually* ....

30.4 Complete the sentences with the words from the box.

5 marks

journey run ~~sail~~ get travel trip

Example Liners still regularly ....*sail*.......... across the Atlantic from Europe to New York.

1 People often say that .... broadens the mind but unfortunately it's not always true.
2 Ross planned the trip carefully, making sure that everything would .... smoothly.
3 After arriving at the airport, we still had a long .... through the mountains to our hotel.
4 Maria is away on a business .... at the moment.
5 The train was so crowded that it was impossible to .... a seat.

Your score

/35

31.1

10 marks

Match the words / expressions from the box with the correct definitions.

campsite   caraon   guesthouse   youth hostel   self-catering   ~~tent~~
package holiday   cruise   adventure holiday   excursion   holiday brochure

Example canvas or nylon structure that you pitch and then sleep in   tent

1 holiday where almost everything is paid for in advance
2 holiday on a ship calling at different ports
3 you rent a flat or house and do your own cooking and cleaning
4 special place where people can pitch their tents
5 simple cheap accommodation aimed largely at young people
6 sightseeing trip
7 simple hotel, usually family-run
8 vehicle which you can drive to special places and then sleep in
9 travel company's booklet with information and publicity for their holidays
10 holiday involving unusual, exciting and possibly dangerous activities

31.2

10 marks

Match the words with the correct definitions / synonyms.

Example unique   [f]

1 breathtaking   ☐
2 exhilarating   ☐
3 exclusive   ☐
4 exotic   ☐
5 glamorous   ☐
6 luxurious   ☐
7 picturesque   ☐
8 unspoilt   ☐
9 impressive   ☐
10 memorable   ☐

a unusual, very different from your everyday life
b providing great comfort
c so special it will never be forgotten
d grand, making a strong impact
e still in a beautiful and natural state
f nothing else like it
g makes you feel full of energy
h for only a limited number of special people
i stunning, magnificent
j exciting and attractive
k pretty as a picture

31.3

10 marks

Which adjective collocates better with each noun?

Example a village – *remote or terrifying?* a remote village

1 a road – *winding* or *surrounding?*
2 a nightclub – *unspoilt* or *exclusive?*
3 charm – *picturesque* or *luxurious?*
4 a climb – *breathtaking* or *exclusive?*
5 a museum – *fascinating* or *glamorous?*
6 food – *exceptional* or *unspoilt?*
7 a lifestyle – *picturesque* or *luxurious?*
8 an opportunity – *unique* or *inconvenient?*
9 holiday – *memorable* or *breathtaking?*
10 countryside – *surrounding* or *winding?*

31.4

5 marks

Complete the sentences with the correct form of the words in brackets.

Example We spent a ....delightful......... time in the south of France. (delight)

1 Holiday brochures tend to .... the locations they describe. (glamour)
2 Unfortunately our hotel was rather .... located. (convenient)
3 I had a wonderful feeling of .... when I reached the top of the hill. (exhilarate)
4 Our cabin was quite .... with ordinary rather than bunk beds. (luxury)
5 I think it was one of the most .... holidays I've ever had. (memory)

Your score
/35

Science and technology

32.1

Match the verbs from the box with the correct definitions.

> dissect   rotate   extract   combine   insert   ~~conclude~~
> utilise   analyse   install   flash   experiment

Example come to a decision after thinking carefully about it *conclude*

1 turn, go round (e.g. of wheel) ....
2 make use of ....
3 take out, remove ....
4 shine suddenly and brightly ....
5 study or examine in detail ....
6 join together ....
7 put something inside something else ....
8 try something in order to find out some information ....
9 put a computer program into a computer so that the computer can use it ....
10 cut open something in order to study its structure ....

32.2

Complete the sentences with the correct forms of the words in brackets.

Example Jake gave his parents a ....*digital*......... photo frame for their anniversary. (digit)

1 Genetic .... is an increasingly important academic discipline. (engine)
2 Claire is studying .... biology at university. (molecule)
3 Voice technology .... people to operate machines by speaking to them. (able)
4 Cloning is the .... of exact copies of plants or animals. (create)
5 GM stands for .... -modified. (gene)
6 Chemistry and geology are .... branches of science. (tradition)

32.3

Label the pictures with the words from the box.

> tablet   smartphone   satnav   digital photo frame   3D TV   HD camcorder

Example ....3D TV............   2 ....   4 ....
1 ....   3 ....   5 ....

32.4

Choose the correct words in these sentences.

Example To operate the machine you need to press this *button* / *disc*.

1 Hydroponics involves growing plants without any *water* / *soil*.
2 Dissection helps medical students learn about people's internal *parts* / *organs*.
3 I'm afraid there is a fundamental *flaw* / *failure* in your *problem* / *theory*.
4 She was surprised by the way the *chemists* / *chemicals reacted* / *pulled* when they were combined.
5 *Cloning* / *Ergonomics* focuses on the effective use of working *space* / *area*.
6 Pull this *lever* / *disk* when you want to start the machine.
7 Genetic engineering allows scientists to *alter* / *associate* features in people's *DNA* / *GM*.
8 Researchers are involved in a number of interesting new *branches* / *roots* of science these days.
9 Science is increasingly able to modify the *construction* / *structure* of human *software* / *cells*.

33.1 Put the jumbled letters in the correct order to make words matching the definitions.

10 marks

Example piece of equipment that lets you copy pictures onto your computer
RANSCEN   *scanner*

1 a large unit of computer memory   BAGGYTIE
2 a small portable computer   POLPAT
3 what you look at on your computer   SIDYALP
4 a program that lets you work with information in rows and columns   SHATEDEPERS
5 a flashing mark on your computer screen that shows you where text will appear if you start typing   ROCURS
6 computer programs   WOSTFEAR
7 a way of storing information about, e.g. customers, on a computer ABETSADA
8 pictures and images on a computer   CHARPIGS
9 piece of equipment, tool   EVIDEC
10 set of connected computers   KNOWERT

33.2 Read the statements. Tick True or False.

10 marks

	True	False
Example App is short for *appliance*.	☐	☑
1 A virus helps your computer work more efficiently.	☐	☐
2 A *microchip* is a very small device which enables your computer to perform particular operations.	☐	☐
3 *RAM* stands for *random access microchip*.	☐	☐
4 *Hardware* is a term used to refer to computer equipment.	☐	☐
5 A scanner lets you analyse figures in a computer program.	☐	☐
6 A tablet is usually operated by a mouse.	☐	☐
7 Large amounts of information are stored on a hard drive.	☐	☐
8 *PC* stands for *private computer*.	☐	☐
9 Screen pictures which represent programs are known as *icons*.	☐	☐
10 A group of connected computers are said to be *networked*.	☐	☐

33.3 Correct the false statements from 33.2.

5 marks

Example App is short for *application*.

33.4 Complete the sentences with the words from the box. (You may need to change the form.)

10 marks

> store   back up   upgrade   ~~install~~   key in   click   delete   crash   undo   download   plug

Example It took a long time to ....*install*........ the software but it's working well now.

1 Your essay is good but rather long. I think you should .... the middle section.
2 It's important to .... your work every day. You could lose it if your computer ....
3 I'm going to have to .... my computer because it doesn't have enough memory to run some of the software I have to use for work.
4 People nowadays tend to .... music and films rather than buying CDs or DVDs.
5 To get onto the website you'll have to .... this password.
6 To open the program, just .... on this icon.
7 I've bought a separate small hard drive where I .... all my photos.
8 .... a memory stick into my computer and take a copy of my presentation.
9 Most computer programs allow you to .... a mistake you have just made.

Your score
/35

Communications and the Internet

34.1

Complete the sentences with the words from the box.

| access | attach | browse | down | enter | Google | in | keep | ~~send~~ | Skype | subscribe |

Example Don't forget to ....send......... Helen an e-card for her birthday.

1 When you email me back, remember to .... some of your holiday photos.
2 If you don't .... your user information correctly, you won't be able to log on.
3 You come across a lot of interesting information when you .... the net.
4 Lena and George .... their grandchildren in Australia every Sunday.
5 I feel quite lost when the server is .... and I can't use the Internet.
6 If you want to check any information, the easiest thing is to .... it.
7 Broadband connections have made it much faster to .... information on the Internet.
8 You won't be able to log .... to this site unless you .... to it first.
9 Facebook makes it easy for people to .... in touch with their friends.

34.2

Match the words on the left with those on the right to form compound nouns. (Some will be written as one word and some as two.)

Example network

service virtual
~~net~~
social user broad home
contact
book pass online

list band name
reality page networking
word gaming ~~work~~
provider mark

34.3

Match the beginning of each sentence with its ending.

Example A wireless network means you don't need [g]   a to navigate around.
1 Don't forget to bookmark ☐   b blogs I regularly read.
2 An interactive website allows users ☐   c to subscribe to some sites.
3 A good website makes it easy for users ☐   d to contribute to it.
4 Hari writes one of the very few ☐   e links to other pages.
5 You have to pay if you want ☐   f sites you use frequently.
6 The home pages give you ☐   g cables to get Internet
                            access.

34.4

Complete the sentences with the correct words.

Example It's easy to waste a lot of time on your computer surfing the ....web........... .

1 I think Google is probably my favourite search ....
2 ISP stands for internet service ....
3 Wikipedia, as its name suggests, is an example of a type of interactive website known as a ....
4 If you don't have a password for the site, you won't be able to log ....
5 I'm sending my CV with this email as an ....
6 When you leave the bank's secure website, it is important to remember to log ....
7 The magazine article resulted in our website experiencing a record number of ....
8 You can't see each other when you're Skyping unless you both have a ....
9 FAQ stands for frequently asked ....

The press and the media

35.1
10 marks

Correct the mistakes in these sentences.

Example Grandma loves reading about political ~~scandalous~~. scandals

1 Many of the articles in tablet newspapers are about TV and pop stars.
2 *Neighbours* is a popular Australian soup.
3 That magazine publishes some very good in-deep articles about the economy.
4 Satellite discs are useful but can look very ugly on the sides of houses.
5 Popular newspapers are more interested in sensitivity than real news.
6 Which is your preferred mean of communication?
7 My cousin has just got a great job as a present on a TV breakfast show.
8 John loves watching programmes about currency affairs.
9 Serious newspapers are also sometimes referred to as quantity papers.
10 I hate it when a good film on TV is constantly interrupted by commercialists.

35.2
10 marks

Complete the sentences with the correct forms of the verbs in the box.

| televise | ~~broadcast~~ | shoot | tweet | investigate | dub |
| receive | stream | focus | subscribe | be | |

Example Tonight's concert ...*will be broadcast*... live on TV and radio.

1 I prefer watching .... foreign films rather than ones with sub-titles.
2 We have a satellite dish which enables us to .... all sorts of foreign TV stations.
3 You can only watch those football matches live if you have .... to a special TV channel.
4 Come and watch TV – the news .... just about to start.
5 Rob joined Twitter so he could read what his favourite footballers .... about.
6 They'll .... the prince's wedding but you can listen to it on the radio as well.
7 Use the Internet to .... a live TV programme and watch it on your laptop.
8 I saw an interesting documentary .... what goes into fast food.
9 The first programme in the series .... on healthcare in the USA.
10 The film .... on location in Italy two years ago.

35.3
10 marks

Match the categories from the box with the programme descriptions.

Example 9 o'clock headlines – what's happened today *news*

1 **Ruth and Friends** – Ruth chats to guests
2 **Family Challenge** – families compete to win prizes
3 **The next five days** – the latest meteorological predictions
4 **Ramsay Square** – daily drama from the square
5 **Mickey and Dave** – two rabbit heroes travel in space
6 **Match of the Day** – the day's main football events
7 **Birds of the Jungle** – film of the Amazon river
8 **Inspector Friendly** – a mysterious murder
9 **Tyler Twins** – hilarious series about identical twins
10 **Worldview** – investigating the growth of Internet crime

| cartoon |
| game show |
| detective drama |
| ~~news~~ |
| sitcom |
| soap |
| sports show |
| talk show |
| weather forecast |
| wildlife documentary |
| current affairs programme |

35.4
5 marks

Complete the sentences with the correct words. (The first letters are given.)

Example To work on this newspaper, you need experience as well as a degree in j o u r n a l i s m

1 They're s _ _ _ _ _ _ that film you said you wanted to see at the Odeon tonight. Shall we go?
2 I don't use that website now that you have to pay a s _ _ _ _ _ _ _ _ _ _ _.
3 I like to download some p _ _ _ _ _ _ _ to listen to on my journey to work.
4 I'm reading a very interesting book about the impact of the m _ _ _ media.
5 I very much enjoyed the first e _ _ _ _ _ _ of that new drama last night.

36.1 Complete the sentences with the words from the box.

10 marks

> nominate judge chamber ~~democracy~~ cast seat
> legislature stand politician head polling

Example ...*Democracy*... is sometimes defined as government of the people, for the people, by the people.

1 The day of an election, the day when people .... their vote for the .... of their choice, is also known as .... day.
2 The Prime Minister is the .... of the Cabinet of Ministers.
3 Julia is planning to .... for Parliament in the next election. Her father had a .... in the House of Commons for many years.
4 It is the role of the President of this country to .... the person who will act as senior .... in the supreme court.
5 The House of Commons can also be referred to as the lower ....
6 The .... of a country is the group of people whose role it is to make and change laws.

36.2 Put the words from the box in the correct columns.

10 marks

> Congress Prime Minister ~~House of Lords~~ Senate monarch MP Parliament
> President representative House of Commons House of Representatives

US	UK
	House of Lords

36.3 Which word is being defined? (The first letters are given.)

5 marks

Example a person competing for an elected position a c a n d i d a t e

1 to make a choice   to s _ _ _ _ _
2 to be in charge of   to h _ _ _
3 people indicate their vote on this   a b _ _ _ _ _ p _ _ _ _
4 the period for which a person is elected   his or her t _ _ _ of office
5 a state governed by representatives and led by a president   a r _ _ _ _ _ _ _

36.4 Complete the sentences with words formed from the words in brackets.

10 marks

Example An MP is the ...*representative*... of his or her constituency in Parliament. (represent)

1 July 4th is celebrated as .... Day in the USA. (depend)
2 This country holds a general .... every five years. (elect)
3 The Party will publish its economic and social .... in a manifesto next week. (politics)
4 The Labour Party currently has a small .... in Parliament. (major)
5 The UK is one of the few countries still ruled as a .... (monarch)
6 The USA is a .... of fifty states and one district. (federal)
7 A .... is a country run by one all-powerful, unelected ruler. (dictate)
8 Introducing a law like that at this point would be .... unwise. (politics)
9 Tell me about the system of .... in your country. (govern)
10 The next .... election will be in two years' time. (preside)

Your score

/35

37.1 Choose the correct words in these sentences.
10 marks

Example A *jury* / judge is a group of citizens who decide whether an accused person is guilty or not.

1 Kidnapping is a very serious *offender / offence*.
2 Sam Brown will be *tried / trialled* for burglary next month.
3 The *defence / prosecuting* lawyer was able to make use of a great deal of evidence against the accused.
4 After long *deliveries / deliberations* the jury came to their decision.
5 The jury decided that the man had not committed the crime and was *guilty / innocent*.
6 The judge's role is to decide on an appropriate *verdict / punishment* for criminals.
7 People who are the *victim / object* of a crime may be offered professional support.
8 The lawyer said that the Richardson robbery was a particularly difficult *case / process*.
9 The crime was planned by Jones who used Blake as his *helper / accomplice*.
10 The police are sure Hamilton is guilty but have no *investigation / proof*.

37.2 Which word is being defined?
6 marks

Example dishonestly taking something which belongs to someone else and keeping it *theft*

1 taking items from a shop without paying ....
2 killing someone ....
3 taking someone's child and then asking the parents for money ....
4 acting violently for political purposes ....
5 stealing from someone's house ....
6 taking something illegally into another country ....

37.3 Complete the text with the correct forms of the words in the box.
14 marks

| arrest | charge | ~~commit~~ | court | evidence | plead | prison |
| release | rob | sentence | serve | steal | time | trial | verdict |

Jake ...*committed*... a crime when he (1) .... a post office. He (2) ....
£10,000. A witness managed to take a photo of him leaving the scene of the crime. The
police (3) .... him and (4) .... him with robbery. The case was heard in
(5) .... three months later. At his (6) .... Jake (7) .... not guilty.
However, the photograph was used in (8) .... against him, and, as a result, the
jury passed a (9) .... of guilty. The judge (10) .... him to ten years in
(11) .... Jake (12) .... eight years but was then (13) .... ,
having got (14) .... off for good behaviour.

37.4 Underline the stressed syllable in the words in bold.
5 marks

Example Smith was con**vic**ted for shoplifting.

1 The police **suspected** Sarah of stealing the money.
2 The **convicts** were set to work in the mines.
3 Paul was asked a lot of questions about the crime but is not a **suspect**.
4 The police are hopeful that the accused will be **convicted**.
5 The man I told the police about is now their main **suspect**.

38.1 Complete the dialogue with the words from the box.

> cash charges ~~current~~ debit deposit loan
> mortgage overdrawn outgoings pay salaries

CHILD: What do you use the bank for?
MUM: Well, we have a ......*current*...... account where we pay in our monthly (1) ....
Then we can use money from that account to (2) .... any bills.
CHILD: What if you spend more than you've got?
MUM: Well, if your (3) .... are more than your income, you're (4) .... and
the bank usually (5) .... you interest.
CHILD: What else do banks do?
MUM: Well, you can get a bank (6) .... if you want to borrow a large sum of money.
CHILD: To buy a house, for example?
MUM: That's right. That's usually called a (7) ....
CHILD: How do you pay the bank back?
MUM: Well, for something big like a house, you usually have to pay a (8) ....
first. Then you pay the rest back in instalments every month. We pay by direct
(9) .... which means a transfer is made from our account automatically.
CHILD: And if you want some actual money from your account?
MUM: Well, I usually just go to a (10) .... machine.

38.2 What is the difference between ...

Example an *account in credit* and an *account in the red?* an account in credit has money in
it; an account in the red is overdrawn (= owes money to the bank)

1 ... *income* and *outgoings?*   3 ... a *current account* and a *savings account?*
2 ... *inheritance tax* and *corporation tax?*   4 ... a *debt* and a *payment?*

38.3 Complete the sentences with the correct words.

Example Your debit card allows you to get money from a cash ......*machine*...... abroad.

1 *VAT* stands for *value added* ....
2 Shops at airports or on ships where you don't pay tax on purchases are called
.... -free shops.
3 *To start a new bank account* is usually called *to* .... *an account.*
4 The amount of interest that a bank charges on loans or pays on savings is known as the
interest ....
5 If you buy a car, you should explore different ways of .... your purchase.
6 A .... card allows you to pay for things at a later date.
7 Stan's new job involves helping to .... money for a children's charity.
8 Customs duty which is paid on items brought into a country is also known as .... duty.
9 It is better to .... many loans into one so you just have one payment each month.
10 If the bank gives you an overdraft .... , you are allowed to go into the red.
11 *To* .... *money* is to move it from one account to another.
12 A .... income is one that comes in in a regular and reliable way.

38.4 Complete the sentences with words formed from the words in brackets.

Example Heirs have to pay ...*inheritance*... tax after a death. (inherit)

1 The bank claims to offer very .... rates of interest. (compete)
2 We have to budget for a couple of loan .... every month. (repay)
3 I find online .... very convenient, don't you? (bank)
4 The bank always charges heavily for an .... (overdraw)
5 The company will pay back any .... you incur on a business trip but you must keep
your receipts. (spend)

39.1 Match the opposites.

10 marks

Example thick – thin

thick   strong
genuine
conventional   decorative   stiff
transparent   vivid
natural   delicate
faulty

perfect   opaque
weak   sombre   tough
artificial   thin
flexible   fake   plain
bizarre

39.2 Complete the table.

6 marks

adjective	noun
entire	entirety
solid	
	decency
precise	
	character
severe	
	triviality

39.3 Choose the correct words to complete these sentences.

13 marks

Example This painting isn't by Van Gogh; it's *genuine* / *fake*.

1 Plastic is a more *stiff* / *flexible* material than steel.
2 It's important to take *precise* / *imprecise* measurements when making a dress.
3 Some people criticise the artist's work for being too *sincere* / *trivial*.
4 Grace's grandpa has just had an operation to give him *a natural* / *an artificial* hip.
5 The room was decorated in a *plain* / *solid* but tasteful way.
6 Be careful with that vase – it's quite *weak* / *fragile*.
7 The coffee machine I bought yesterday is *faulty* / *perfect* – I'm going to return it.
8 I wouldn't jump on the bed if I were you – it doesn't look very *delicate* / *sturdy*.
9 Suzie usually wears *vivid* / *sombre* red, purple or orange clothes.
10 The painting is *conventional* / *characteristic* of Picasso's later period.
11 It's hard to get a *decent* / *transparent* cup of coffee in this town.
12 Julia has just eaten an *entire* / *opaque* box of chocolates.
13 The sculpture is *bizarre* / *tough* but still beautiful.

39.4 Put the words in the right order to make sentences.

6 marks

Example don't / coffee / This / strong, / is / agree? / unusually / you
   This coffee is unusually strong, don't you agree?

1 isn't / writer's / her / latest / The / half / interesting / book / as / one. / first / as
2 good / in / reasonably / opinion. / a / It's / my / hotel, /
3 big / has / his / a / Andy / bruise / leg. / on / great / got
4 strong. / father / unusually / likes / tea / My / his
5 nowhere / motorbike / her / Hilly's / is / as / near / boyfriend's. / powerful / as
6 lot / a / have / books / pretty / to / of / our / thick / course. / for / read / We

40.1 Match each phrase on the left with the best paraphrase on the right.

10 marks

Example In my view   b   a I do not think that it is true

1 I'm convinced that ☐   b In my opinion

2 I maintain ☐   c I believe even if it seems doubtful

3 I have my doubts about ☐   d I have a strong feeling something isn't right

4 I've always held that ☐   e I believe most strongly that

5 I reckon ☐   f I have some worries about

6 I'm in favour of ☐   g I have consistently believed that

7 I feel ☐   h I am for

8 I'm against ☐   i I have a strong, personal opinion or sense

9 I suspect that ☐   j I'm opposed to

10 I doubt that ☐   k I guess or estimate

40.2 Find pairs of synonyms.

5 marks

Example obsessive – fanatical

committed   conservative   ~~obsessive~~   eccentric   extreme   moderate
middle-of-the-road   ~~fanatical~~   dedicated   radical   traditional   odd

40.3 Complete the sentences with the correct prepositions.

10 marks

Example Was the Prime Minister right to act as he did, ...*in*.. your opinion?

1 Are you for or .... capital punishment?

2 From a practical point .... view, your proposal makes good sense.

3 An atheist doesn't believe .... any god.

4 Alastair holds some rather eccentric views .... marriage.

5 What do you think .... Priya's new flat?

6 Petra has some doubts .... how sincere Ben is.

7 Are you .... favour .... the proposal?

8 I'm opposed .... any kind of military intervention.

9 .... my view, you're making a serious mistake.

40.4 What do we call ...

10 marks

Example ... a person who believes in the scientific theories of Charles Darwin? ..*a Darwinist*..

1 ... a person who refuses to fight in any war and believes in non-violence?

....

2 ... a person who doesn't eat meat? ....

3 ... a person who believes in socialism? ....

4 ... a follower of Islam? ....

5 ... views that tend to be against change? c.....................

6 ... the opposite of right-wing? ....

7 ... the opposite of extreme views? m.....................

8 ... values that relate to standards of what is good or bad behaviour?

m.....................

9 ... relating to the ability to think and understand things, especially complicated
ideas? i.....................

10 ... relating to a philosophy that concerns a single individual rather than a group?

p.....................

Your score

/35

Pleasant and unpleasant feelings

41.1 Read the statements and tick True or False.   True   False

10 marks

Example If you feel contented, you feel satisfied with how things are in your life. ✓ ☐

1 When you are anxious, you feel confident that things will go well. ☐ ☐
2 You feel frustrated when you want to do something but can't do it. ☐ ☐
3 If you are, for example, enthusiastic about an idea, you are keen on the idea. ☐ ☐
4 If things turn out as you'd hoped, you feel miserable. ☐ ☐
5 If you are very pleased about, for example, an exam result, you could say
   you are delighted with it. ☐ ☐
6 If someone does something that is very kind and helpful, you feel grateful to them. ☐ ☐
7 When you are looking forward to something special like a long holiday, you
   feel upset. ☐ ☐
8 When you feel relieved and pleased that things happened better than they
   might have done, you feel thankful. ☐ ☐
9 When things are going well for someone, they usually feel depressed. ☐ ☐
10 Sometimes people bite their nails when they are nervous. ☐ ☐

41.2 Match the adjectives in the box with each speaker's feelings.

5 marks

| confused   content   furious   ~~fed up~~   discontented   inspired |

Example I don't seem to be doing anything but work at the moment. I really need a break!
          fed up

1 Look at that wonderful rainbow! I must write a poem! ....
2 He should never have behaved towards you like that. It's disgraceful! ....
3 I know I don't have any real problems but somehow I don't feel fulfilled either at work or
   with my social life. ....
4 I love my little flat. I never want to live anywhere else now. ....
5 I just don't know what to think. One minute everything seems fine, the next it's all going
   wrong again. ....

41.3 Does *quite* mean *totally* or *rather* in each of these phrases?

10 marks

Example quite anxious = *rather anxious*

1 quite depressed   6 quite inspired
2 quite delighted   7 quite nervous
3 quite enthusiastic   8 quite sick and tired
4 quite furious   9 quite thrilled
5 quite grateful   10 quite upset

41.4 Write the adjectives for these nouns.

10 marks

Example delight ....*delighted*....

1 anxiety ....   6 depression ....
2 enthusiasm .... 7 fury ....
3 gratitude ....   8 thankfulness ....
4 inspiration .... 9 confusion ....
5 thrill ....   10 nervousness ....

Your score

/35

Like, dislike and desire

42.1 Rewrite the sentences to mean the same, using the words in brackets.

10 marks

Example We loved each other the first time our eyes met. (fell)
We fell in love the first time our eyes met.

1 I strongly disapprove of his behaviour. (appals)
2 It's been so difficult at work. I can't wait for my holiday. (longing)
3 Maria likes romantic novels very much. (fond)
4 Amy didn't fancy Ben. (attractive)
5 He loves his daughter more than anyone else in the world. (cares)
6 I detest standing in queues. (bear)
7 I loathe violent films. (disgust)
8 I always hate the thought of going back to work after a holiday. (dread)
9 I find his enthusiasm and energy attractive. (appeal)
10 Paddy despises his new boss. (stand)

42.2 Complete the text with the correct prepositions.

10 marks

As soon as Ramona set eyes .....*on*..... Alex, she fell [(1)] .... love [(2)] .... him. She was captivated [(3)] .... his beautiful smile and his kindness to everyone he cared [(4)] .... His sense of humour also appealed [(5)] .... her, as did the way he was passionate [(6)] .... his work. She had been looking [(7)] .... [(8)] .... going on holiday but, once she had fallen [(9)] .... him, she was no longer keen [(10)] .... going away on her own.

42.3 Read the statements and tick True or False. Use a dictionary if necessary.

5 marks

	True	False
Example Kleptomaniacs experience a desire to break things.	☐	✓
1 Marxists are passionate about Groucho Marx.	☐	☐
2 Sadists dread causing pain.	☐	☐
3 Claustrophobics can't stand Christmas.	☐	☐
4 Ornithologists are fascinated by horns.	☐	☐
5 Misogynists can't stand unmarried women.	☐	☐

42.4 Correct the false statements in 42.3.

5 marks

Example Kleptomaniacs experience a desire to steal things.

42.5 Put the words in the correct column.

5 marks

~~desire~~ fascinated repel yearn affectionate revolt

liking	disliking
desire	

43.1 Complete the sentences with the correct forms of the verbs in the box.

10 marks

> beg boast complain confess grumble insist
> murmur ~~scream~~ stutter threaten urge

Example 'There's a mouse. I can't stand mice,' she .....screamed..... .

1 'I'll contact my lawyer if you lay a finger on my daughter,' he ....
2 'I c-c-c-can't h-h-help you,' .... Bob.
3 'I'm far better than the other students in my class,' Victoria ....
4 'You really must be here by 8,' the teacher ....
5 'I'm afraid I read your diary,' he ....
6 'You're the most beautiful girl in the world,' he .... in her ear.
7 'My glass is dirty,' she ....
8 'Please, please, lend me the money,' he ....
9 'I don't want to do my homework,' .... the child.
10 'Just have one more try. You're nearly there,' .... the boy's mother.

43.2 Rewrite the sentences in 43.1 replacing each verb with *said* + the most appropriate
10 marks adverb from the box below. Make any necessary changes to word order.

> angrily crossly desperately encouragingly firmly
> furiously guiltily ~~loudly~~ nervously proudly softly

Example 'There's a mouse. I can't stand mice,' she .....said loudly..... .

43.3 Complete each sentence with the correct preposition(s) and the appropriate form of
9 marks the verb in brackets (either an infinitive or an *-ing* form).

Example I haven't spoken to my parents yet .....about changing.. my course. (change)

1 My aunt insisted .... me a present (buy)
2 I really object .... people .... in my house. (smoke)
3 They are always grumbling .... to work on Sundays. (have)
4 The accused has never confessed .... the murder. (commit)
5 He begged me .... money and then begged me .... him find
  somewhere to live. (help)
6 Mark complained .... his boss .... his colleague ....
  the sack. (get)
7 Jo has threatened .... an official complaint ....
  her boss if things don't improve. (make)
8 Harriet is always arguing .... her parents .... her
  room. (tidy)
9 Will Brad ever stop boasting .... first prize. (win)

43.4 Is the person most likely to be feeling *angry*, *happy* or *sad* if they speak in these ways?
6 marks
Example cheerfully happy

1 gloomily ....
2 bitterly ....
3 miserably ....
4 gladly ....
5 furiously ....
6 hopefully ....

Your score
/35

The six senses

44.1
10 marks
Which sense do each of these verbs or adjectives go with: *sight, hearing, taste, touch* or *smell*?

gaze sight	deafening	glimpse	mild taste	silent	putrid
salty	poke	spicy	stinking	tap	witness

44.2
11 marks
Complete the sentences with the correct forms of the verbs from the box.

> glance grab grasp handle notice observe
> peer poke press stare pat ~~witness~~

Example The police are anxious to talk to anyone who ......*witnessed*.... the accident.

1 Now, class, I'd like you to note down all the birds you .... in your garden next weekend.
2 Look at that man over there. Why is he .... at us?
3 Maddy bent down to .... the dog that had just brought her its ball.
4 If you want to stop the machine, just .... the red button at the top.
5 This glass has great sentimental value for me, so please .... it carefully.
6 I was surprised when I .... out of the window and saw it was snowing.
7 The fire bell's ringing – just .... your handbag and leave the building.
8 .... me in the ribs if you .... I've fallen asleep in the lecture.
9 When no one answered the door, Jiro .... through the letterbox trying to see into the flat.
10 Now children, ... your partner's hand firmly, and we'll all cross the road carefully together.

44.3
4 marks
Match the words on the left with the examples on the right.

Example sixth sense [c]
1 telepathy [ ]
2 premonition [ ]
3 déjà vu [ ]
4 intuition [ ]

a dreaming about an accident before it happens
b thinking about a friend a second before she rings you
c having any of the experiences in this exercise
d sensing why a close friend is upset
e walking into a place and feeling you've been there before

44.4
10 marks
Make complete sentences with the verbs and phrases in the table.

Example Alicia has won a holiday to Bali. She feels very excited.

~~Alicia has won a holiday to Bali. She~~		
1 This curry needs more spices. I think it		very pleasant. too sweet. so soft.
2 Anna is going on a diet. She is slim but thinks she		
3 Do you think he's going to be sick? He	feels	~~very excited.~~
4 Have you heard about the trip to Nepal? It	looks	fat.
5 Here comes the bride. She	smells	too mild.
6 I haven't met Sam's new teacher yet but she	sounds	so fragrant.
7 I love stroking the cat. It	tastes	wonderful.
8 I love this rose. It		rather green.
9 No one has lived in this house for ages. It		musty
10 They've put too much chocolate in this cake. It		very exciting.

What your body does

45.1
Match the verbs with the correct definitions.

Example blink [i]   a smile broadly

1 bite [ ]   b noise a hungry stomach makes
2 blush [ ]   c cut through something with your teeth
3 perspire [ ]   d deep breath exhaled when relieved or unhappy
4 breathe [ ]   e heavy breathing noise made when asleep
5 grin [ ]   f use lungs to take in air and to exhale
6 rumble [ ]   g close one eye
7 shiver [ ]   h go red
8 sigh [ ]   i open and close both eyes rapidly
9 snore [ ]   j tremble with cold
10 wink [ ]   k sweat

45.2
Which is the odd one out? Explain why.

Example cough, frown, sigh, yawn *'frown' isn't connected with breathing*

1 chew, lick, rumble, suck
2 shake, shiver, tremble, sigh
3 blink, blush, wink, frown
4 cough, grin, shiver, sneeze
5 sweat, snore, cough, rumble

45.3
These sentences have got muddled. Match the endings in italics with the correct beginnings.

Example Suck this sweet ~~because her children are behaving so badly~~.
Suck this sweet to stop your ears popping as the plane descends.

1 Drink this water *because his hands are trembling.*
2 Having had so little sleep last night, *you digest it more easily.*
3 If you chew your food well, *you can get the dust out of your eye.*
4 She's frowning *he's been yawning all day.*
5 Some people sneeze *and you won't feel so nervous.*
6 She sighed with relief *if they come into contact with a cat.*
7 Try blinking to see if *whenever she's embarrassed.*
8 You can tell that he's nervous *when she heard that Nick had arrived safely.*
9 She always blushes ~~to stop your ears popping as the plane descends~~.
10 Take a couple of deep breaths *to help you swallow the pill.*

45.4
Answer these questions about word grammar.

Example What is the noun from the verb *wink*? *a wink*

1 What is the verb from the noun *breath*? ....
2 What are the past tense and the past participle of *bite*? ....
3 What is the noun from the verb *grin*? ....
4 What are the past tense and the past participle of *shake*? ....
5 What is the noun from the verb *perspire*? ....

46.1 Put the words / phrases in the correct columns.

10 marks

> at fault   on the ball   out of this world   pick holes in
> run down   streets ahead   take the biscuit   to blame
> top-notch   want to have your cake and eat it   have a way with

praising	criticising
	at fault

46.2 Correct the mistakes in these sentences.

10 marks

Example Nathan is really ~~in~~ the ball when it comes to figures. on

1 Emma is head and neck above the other pupils at French.
2 Markus is a great gardener – he truly has colourful fingers.
3 They say that people from that part of the world have the gift of the gabble.
4 Toby has a very high opinion of himself; he thinks he's the cat's paws.
5 The film was absolutely first-mark – totally absorbing.
6 I can't understand why Becky thinks she's the bee's stripes.
7 When it comes to punctuation, I'm the world's worse.
8 My little boy is along the best in his class at reading.
9 Tanya's kilometres better than me at swimming.
10 It was annoying to have to pay for the repairs to our car after the accident when we were not with fault.

46.3 Which meaning does *critical* or *critically* have in each sentence? Write: *not pleased, important, giving opinion* or *serious*.

8 marks

Example Kate is at a critical stage in her career. important

1 In their third year, the students have to do a critical review of the literature of the period.
2 It is critical that the Board are all in favour of this course of action.
3 Three men are in a critical condition after the explosion.
4 The film's reviewers were generally very critical of the lead actor's performance.
5 I'm afraid David's grandfather has been critically ill for some time.
6 The author has been critically acclaimed on both sides of the Atlantic.
7 The decisions you make at this stage of your life are critically important.
8 Why do you always have to be so critical of everything I do?

46.4 Choose the correct words in these sentences.

7 marks

Example Chloe has a (way) / manner with children – they always love her.

1 It's *totally* / *highly* absurd to think that your father would agree to give you so much money just to spend on clothes.
2 The teacher praised the children *to* / *for* their hard work.
3 Inge and her sisters all play chess *shiningly* / *brilliantly*.
4 Emily's singing was *highly* / *deeply* praised.
5 The teacher's always *digging* / *picking* holes in my work.
6 I'm afraid that in this life you can't have your *cake* / *biscuit* and eat it.
7 Your English is *roads* / *streets* ahead of the other students'.

Your score

/35

Emotions and moods

47.1 Write P (positive emotion or mood) or N (negative emotion or mood).

10 marks

Example under the weather N

1 on top form
2 scared out of your wits
3 be done in
4 as fit as a fiddle
5 on cloud nine
6 down in the dumps
7 in high spirits
8 on top of the world
9 jump out of your skin
10 to look up

47.2 Complete the phrases to mean the same as the words in brackets. (The first letters are given.)

10 marks

Example I was shaking in my b o o t s as I waited for my exam results. (very frightened)

1 Simon's like a b _ _ _ with a sore head this morning. (very irritable)
2 I feel as if I'm at death's d _ _ _. (very ill)
3 I felt scared s _ _ _ _ during the film. (very afraid)
4 We were all shaking in our s _ _ _ _ as we waited to see the headteacher. (very nervous)
5 The children were as happy as the day is l _ _ _ all summer. (extremely happy)
6 Keep calm – there's no need to throw a w _ _ _ _ _ _ . (get very angry and upset)
7 Alec always keeps a c _ _ _ head in a crisis. (stays calm)
8 Keep your c _ _ _ up – things aren't that bad. (stay positive)
9 Ana's parents s _ _ _ _ _ _ with pride as they watched her win the cup. (felt extremely proud)
10 The bang frightened the l _ _ _ out of me. (made me extremely scared)

47.3 Match each expression with its meaning.

10 marks

Example feel as if your head ☐ d   a deal calmly with events
         is spinning   as they happen

1 get carried away ☐   b feeling good
2 down in the dumps ☐   c feeling cross
3 shake in your boots ☐   d feel dizzy
4 have a long face ☐   e extremely happy
5 take things as they come ☐   f exhausted
6 on top form ☐   g react in a very nervous way
7 in a bad mood ☐   h feel very nervous and apprehensive
8 done in ☐   i lose touch with reality
9 jump out of your skin ☐   j miserable
10 on cloud nine ☐   k a depressed expression

47.4 Rewrite the sentences using the words in brackets.

5 marks

Example Chris looks a bit miserable. (dumps)
        Chris looks a bit down in the dumps.

1 Fatima's not feeling very well. (weather)
2 Mona gets very upset if she doesn't get her own way. (throws)
3 Ian is doing his best to stay cheerful. (chin)
4 All the children are feeling lively and happy. (spirits)
5 The children were very frightened. (wits)

Your score

/35

Commenting on problematic situations

48.1 Complete the sentences with the phrases from the box.

10 marks

> ~~troubled waters~~   take notice   the hatchet   a turning point   the bottom of things
> under the carpet   a dead end   a grasp   our act together   the tide   the end of the tunnel

Example Peacemakers always try to pour oil on ......*troubled waters*....... .

1 The two sides have buried .... and stopped arguing with each other.
2 I'm afraid we've come to .... I don't know what to do to solve the problem.
3 I've been trying to get .... of the situation but I can't make any sense of it.
4 I've sent a very strong protest letter. That should make them sit up and ....
5 The whole problem has just been swept .... Nobody has done anything about it.
6 We're going to have a full investigation to get to ....
7 At last I can see some light at .... – I think we are heading for better times.
8 .... has turned and the economy is growing again now.
9 It's time we got .... and did something about all the complaints.
10 We've reached .... Things are going to be different from now on.

48.2 Correct the preposition mistakes in these sentences.

9 marks

Example Take the bull ~~with~~ the horns and tell Ned what you think of his behaviour.   *by*

1 It must be dreadful to be deprived from your freedom.
2 I'm on a bit of a dilemma at the moment.
3 I can't face the thought about leaving this town.
4 I think we should all lay our cards over the table.
5 I hope everyone will sit down and take notice.
6 We need to do our utmost to get at the bottom of things.
7 Josh has been telling me about the fix he's at.
8 I thought we were making progress but now we seem to have come at a dead end.
9 It's usually better not to try to sweep things below the carpet.

48.3 Choose the correct words in these sentences.

10 marks

Example Raul is in a bit of a *loose/⟨tight⟩* corner and is not sure how he can get out of it.

1 The tornado is the worst *dilemma / disaster* the area has experienced for years.
2 Liz always enjoys *disrupting / stirring* things up at work a bit.
3 Do you think it's true that someone's heart can be *split / broken*?
4 The countryside round here was badly *affected / effected* by last year's storms.
5 I enjoy my work but sometimes I feel it *loses / lacks* a bit of variety.
6 Julian isn't very annoying, just *mildly / intensely* irritating at times.
7 It's supposedly better to think of problems as *disruptions / challenges*.
8 My inclination is always to *take / have* a back seat rather than get involved.
9 I'm afraid my papers are in a bit of a *muddle / corner*.
10 Let me tell you about the dilemma I'm currently *facing / challenging*.

48.4 Complete the table.

6 marks

verb	affect	annoy	irritate		disrupt		deprive
noun	*effect*			collapse		lack	

Your score

/35

Number, quantity, degree and intensity

49.1 Put the words in the correct row.

10 marks

> ~~heaps~~ enormous tons gigantic loads minute
> significant a drop substantial tiny vast

little	
big	heaps

49.2 Complete the sentences with the correct words. (The first letters are given.)

10 marks

Example There has been an e n o r m o u s amount of interest in Salah's new album.

1 There was t _ _ _ of food at Lou's party – I was sorry I'd had dinner first.
2 It takes a c _ _ _ _ _ _ _ _ _ _ _ amount of money to set up your own business.
3 An e _ _ _ _ _ _ _ _ amount of fat in his diet has put him at risk of a heart attack.
4 I've got d _ _ _ _ _ of pencils in my bag if you need to borrow one.
5 I'd like just a d _ _ _ of cream in my coffee, please.
6 Pieter's marks are just a _ _ _ _ _ _, neither very good nor very bad.
7 A s _ _ _ _ _ _ _ _ _ number of students have complained about the cost of the courses.
8 I made l _ _ _ _ of spelling mistakes in my last homework.
9 This newspaper has received s _ _ _ _ _ of letters in response to last Friday's editorial.
10 Matt gave Lisa a look of t _ _ _ _ contempt.

49.3 Complete the sentences with the words from the box.

10 marks

> ban unexpected dependent different disbelief impossible
> inadequate nonsense ~~ridiculous~~ unacceptable chaos

Example Your argument is utterly ....*ridiculous*........ – there's no logic in it at all.

1 They looked at each other in total ....
2 A whole series of signal failures meant that it was utter .... at the railway station this morning.
3 The twins look identical but their personalities are totally ....
4 Alison is so good at everything that she always makes me feel wholly ....
5 Your behaviour is wholly .... – you must apologise at once.
6 What Fran wrote in her essay was utter .... – no wonder it got a terrible mark.
7 There is a total .... on taking food and drink into the classrooms.
8 Whether we go away at the weekend or not will be wholly .... on the weather.
9 I can't do this maths problem at all – it's utterly ....
10 Orla's visit was totally .... but we were all very pleased to see her.

49.4 Complete the sentences by putting the jumbled words in the correct order.

5 marks

Example There's SLOT of work to do before our guests arrive. lots

1 Our English teacher has given us SHAPE of homework to do this evening.
2 I've got SALOD of ideas for things we can do this week.
3 When Carla won the competition she received cards from RECOSS of people she'd never even met.
4 I've got SNOT of work to do today.
5 There's no need to hurry – we've got SGAB of time.

Your score
/35

50.1
10 marks

Label the shapes and lines.

 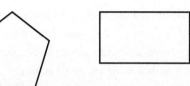

1 ......*square*...... 6 .... 7........................ 9........................

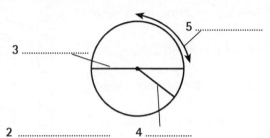 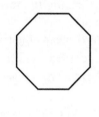 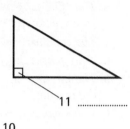

3 ....

5 ....

2 .... 4 .... 8 .... 10 ....

11 ....

50.2
10 marks

Write these numerical expressions in words.

Example $5 \times 9 = 45$ ......*Five times nine equals forty-five.*......

1 $25°\,C$ ....

2 3^2 ....

3 6.8 ....

4 The room is 5m × 7m ....

5 $\frac{9}{10}$ ....

6 6^3 ....

7 41% ....

8 9^7 ....

9 $2,352,796$ ....

10 $2x + 6y$ ....

50.3
10 marks

What is ...

Example ... the noun from the verb *subtract*? subtraction

1 ... the adjective from the noun *circle*?
2 ... the adjective from the noun *sphere*?
3 ... the verb from the noun *multiplication*?
4 ... the adjective from the noun *triangle*?
5 ... the adjective from the noun *oval*?
6 ... the adjective from the noun *spiral*?
7 ... the noun from the verb *divide*?
8 ... the adjective from the noun *octagon*?
9 ... the noun from the verb *add*?
10 ... the adjective from the noun *cube*?

50.4
5 marks

Complete the sentences with the correct words.

Example F in a temperature scale stands for ......*Fahrenheit*...... .

1 Half a circle is a ....
2 Half a sphere is a ....
3 The opposite of *plus* is ....
4 0 in a phone number is usually pronounced ....
5 A pentagon has five ....

Your score

/35

51.1

10 marks

Read the statements and tick True or False.

	True	False
Example The speech lasted for an hour makes it clear that the speaker was bored.	☐	✓
1 *Ten years have elapsed* is more formal than *Ten years have passed.*	☐	☐
2 *It lasts ten hours to fly from Tokyo to Rome* is correct English.	☐	☐
3 The verb *elapse* is used with a wide range of tenses.	☐	☐
4 *My laptop battery lasts about ten hours* is correct English.	☐	☐
5 We say: *This DVD will go for two and a half hours.*	☐	☐
6 *Time flies when you're having fun* means *Time passes more slowly when you're enjoying yourself.*	☐	☐
7 *The train arrived in time* means the train arrived punctually.	☐	☐
8 *Time passes quickly* is correct English.	☐	☐
9 *The meeting dragged on for two hours* suggests that the speaker enjoyed the meeting.	☐	☐
10 *Love makes time pass and time makes love pass* is correct English.	☐	☐

51.2

6 marks

Correct the false statements in 51.1.

Example 'The speech lasted for an hour' is a neutral, factual statement - we don't know whether the speaker was bored or not.

51.3

9 marks

Complete the sentences with the phrases from the box.

| for a time for the time being at times by the time at a time just in time |
| on time from time to time ~~over the course of time~~ time and time again |

Example I know things are difficult now but I'm sure that ...*over the course of time*... it will all get much easier.

1 I got to the airport .... to say goodbye to her.
2 It's your own fault – I've warned you .... to make copies of everything in case the computer crashed!
3 Everyone arrived .... so we were able to start at exactly nine o'clock.
4 The new computer won't arrive until next week. Can you manage with the old one
   .... ?
5 I saw the students one .... in order to give them their results privately.
6 I get very lonely .... [give 2 possibilities].
7 The traffic was terrible. .... I got to the station, the train had left.
8 Although I lived in Athens ...., I never managed to learn Greek.

51.4

10 marks

Choose the correct words in these sentences.

Example We're planning to do the last *age / spell /* (*stage*) of our journey on foot.

1 Richard is writing a book on the history of the Middle *Age / Ages / Eras.*
2 We had a *phase / spell / stage* of good weather in April but it's been dreadful since then.
3 Rome has a *timeless / fleeting / momentary* quality – it will never change.
4 Apart from a couple of *phases / eras / spells* in New York, Joshua worked in Washington.
5 This period has sometimes been referred to as the golden *age / spell / phase* of English poetry.
6 Although the power cut was only *timeless / fleeting / momentary*, it caused problems.
7 The fall of the Berlin Wall marked the end of *an age / an era / a phase.*
8 Many teenagers go through a rebellious *age / era / phase.*
9 We're now going to study the different *ages / stages / eras* in the life of a butterfly.
10 I'm sorry it was such a *timeless / fleeting / momentary* visit – come again for longer soon.

Your score

/35

Distance and dimension

52.1 Complete the table.

10 marks

adjective	verb	noun
long	lengthen	
short		
wide		
deep		
broad		
high		

52.2 Complete the sentences with the correct forms of the nouns or verbs from 52.1.

10 marks

Example The dressmaker suggested ...lengthening.. the dress so that it covered her knees.

1 Maisie decided it was time to .... her horizons and started looking for a job abroad.
2 What is the .... of the swimming pool at the shallow end?
3 At a time of .... emotions, it can be easy to say something you later regret.
4 With cars parked on either side of the road, there is no way something the ....
   of a bus could drive through.
5 Kelly likes to swim twenty .... of the pool every morning before work.
6 I thought my sense of loss would lessen with time but in fact it seems to have ....
7 The sleeves on this jacket are too long – I must get them ....
8 The street is too narrow for so much traffic but they are planning to .... it soon.
9 The school curriculum in this country prides itself mainly on its .... but its
   depth is good too.
10 Kenneth Price was at the .... of his powers in his early forties but things began
   to decline from then on.

52.3 Rewrite the sentences using the correct forms of the verbs in brackets.

5 marks

Example The company's activities have become smaller in recent years. (contract)
   The company's activities have contracted in recent years.

1 There was very rapid growth in the economy last year. (expand)
2 We are planning to build onto our house. (extend)
3 This shirt got smaller when I washed it. (shrink)
4 New houses have been built in the countryside. (spread)
5 The national park covers all the area that you can see from here. (stretch)

52.4 Choose the correct words in these sentences.

10 marks

Example I hope they'll *lower /(raise)* my salary next year.

1 There are some *high / tall* mountains in the north of the country.
2 Louis is already *taller / higher* than his dad.
3 I enjoy travelling to *long / distant* places but my husband is less keen on it.
4 Kenzo is always travelling to *faraway / long-distance* places.
5 I like the way Will is always ready to accept other points of view – he's very *narrow-minded / broad-minded*.
6 Each time the high-jumper successfully jumped over the bar, it was *raised / lowered* another centimetre.
7 You can easily wade across the stream – it's very *broad / shallow*.
8 The little girl opened her eyes *narrow / wide* in amazement.
9 The director gave a *broad / deep* outline of her plans for the company.
10 Draw a rectangle five centimetres *long / low* and three wide.

53.1 Complete the sentences with the correct words. (The first letters are given.)

10 marks

Example We were m <u>a</u> <u>d</u> <u>e</u> to have swimming lessons when I was at school.

1 English is a c _ _ _ _ _ _ _ _ _ subject in most schools in this country.
2 As the concert was cancelled, the organisers were o _ _ _ _ _ _ to give us our money back.
3 A life sentence is m _ _ _ _ _ _ _ _ for anyone who commits murder.
4 You don't have to take that course, it's o _ _ _ _ _ _ _ .
5 Most students are e _ _ _ _ _ from paying tax.
6 We had no a _ _ _ _ _ _ _ _ _ _ but to move to a smaller house.
7 The terrorists f _ _ _ _ _ their victims to lie on the floor.
8 You are l _ _ _ _ _ for any damage you cause to a car you rent.
9 You must take the exam. You have no c _ _ _ _ _ .
10 Military service is o _ _ _ _ _ _ _ _ _ in many countries.

53.2 Rewrite the sentences using the words in brackets.

5 marks

Example Water is a basic thing that human life must have. (necessity)
        Water is an absolute necessity for human life.

1 The country didn't have enough engineers so a foreign company built the road. (shortage)
2 The astronaut died because he didn't have enough oxygen. (lack of)
3 When I got home after being away the lawn needed mowing. (in need)
4 More discussion is needed before we can make a decision. (need for)
5 The garden needs to be watered before we put the new flowers in. (wants)

53.3 Complete the sentences with the correct words.

14 marks

Example There was a 5% rise ....*in*.......... the cost of living last year.

1 I love my iPad and just couldn't do .... it now.
2 What are the requirements .... entry to an engineering course here?
3 The flowers are .... need .... watering.
4 There was .... alternative .... to ask her father for help.
5 If you already have a good knowledge of a foreign language, then you are exempt
   .... this course.
6 Everyone who earns above a certain amount .... liable .... tax.
7 There was no shortage .... volunteers to help at the Games.
8 Frances probably failed her driving test .... lack .... practice.
9 The country has a need .... more male teachers.
10 It's doubtful .... our team will make it through to the next round.

53.4 Complete the sentences with the words from the box.

6 marks

| inevitable   chance   ~~possibility~~   opportunity   probable   certainty   doubtful |

Example All military historians agree that there was little real ....*possibility*.... of the army being
        able to advance at that point.

1 It is .... whether I'll manage to make it home in time for dinner tonight.
2 Is there any .... you could give me a hand tomorrow evening?
3 Our company offers plenty of .... for young graduates.
4 They say that two things in life are .... : death and taxes.
5 It seems .... that there will be a change in government at the next election but it's
   not a ....

Your score

/35

54.1 Put S if the word relates to sound or L if it relates to light.

10 marks

bang	S	chime		flash		flicker		glow		hiss	
hum		rustle		shine		thud		twinkle			

54.2 Choose the correct words in these sentences.

10 marks

Example Screech / Clatter /(Ring) the bell if there is no one at the reception desk.

1 Please don't make so much *sound / noise / patter* – I'm trying to work.
2 The children's faces were *flashing / glowing / humming* with happiness.
3 The brakes *rattled / clanged / screeched* and the car came to a standstill just in time.
4 I could see the *beam / ray / sparkle* from a car's headlights ahead of me.
5 I woke up with the noise of the saucepan *rustling / hissing / crashing* to the floor.
6 The torch needs new batteries – its light is too *dark / sombre / dim* now.
7 The country is so densely populated that you can never escape from the *ring / rumble / thud* of traffic.
8 I love to look at the stars *twinkling / rustling / flashing* in the night sky.
9 Cheer up! Don't look so *dim / dark / gloomy*!
10 Please ask the children to stop that *sound / racket / patter*. I can't hear myself think.

54.3 Match the words on the left with the examples on the right.

8 marks

Example roar [f]

1 clatter ☐   a a balloon as it burst
2 thud ☐   b thunder in the distance
3 bang ☐   c pots and pans being moved in a kitchen
4 hiss ☐   d piles of dry leaves blown by the wind
5 rustle ☐   e rain falling on a metal roof
6 clang ☐   f a jumbo jet taking off
7 rumble ☐   g gas escaping from a pipe
8 patter ☐   h a big heavy object falling onto a stone floor
   i a heavy object falling onto a carpeted floor

54.4 Complete the sentences with the correct words. (The first and last letters are given.)

7 marks

Example The sun s h o n e all day long.

1 The exhibition of ancient treasure was wonderful with jewels s _ _ _ _ _ _ g and gold g _ _ _ _ _ _ _ g all round us.
2 We could hear wedding bells c _ _ _ _ _ g in the distance.
3 She r _ _ _ _ _ d her tin of money and asked us to give something to help the children's hospital.
4 In an open-plan office, there is always a background h _ _ of computers and photocopiers.
5 The candle f _ _ _ _ _ _ _ d in the breeze and then went out.
6 I woke when the first r _ _ s of sunshine came through my window.

55.1 **What are the correct words? (The first letters are given.)**

10 marks

Example What do you call the person that something belongs to? its o <u>w n e r</u>

1 What do you call the person you pay rent to if you live in their house or flat? a l _ _ _ _ _ _
  or a l _ _ _ _ _ _
2 What do you call a person who rents a house or flat from someone else? a t _ _ _ _ _
3 What word describes everything a person owns? their p _ _ _ _ _ _ _ _ _
4 What verb is often used to describe giving money for a good cause? d _ _ _ _ _
5 What word describes the owner of a business like a hotel / shop / newspaper? p _ _ _ _ _ _ _ _
6 What verb means to receive money or other things from someone after their death? i _ _ _ _ _ _
7 What noun can mean either a large area of private land including the buildings on it or all of someone's wealth at their death? e _ _ _ _ _
8 What noun, always in the plural form, is used to mean what a person owns, especially the things which can be carried? b _ _ _ _ _ _ _ _
9 What verb means to support a person or activity by giving money or other help? s _ _ _ _ _ _

55.2 **Complete the sentences with the correct prepositions.**

8 marks

Example Helen has contributed a lot of time and effort ....to......... the project.

1 Don't let go .... my hand or I'll fall.
2 I wish I hadn't given all my old records .... !
3 This holiday resort caters .... all ages.
4 When Fred took over the project, Andy had to hand .... all the files to him.
5 The teacher asked Miranda to hand .... the worksheets to all the students in the class.
6 The students were all supplied .... dictionaries to use in the test.
7 The well was used for centuries to provide water .... the village.
8 I can't provide you .... any more information.

55.3 **Complete the sentences with the correct forms of the verbs from the box.**

10 marks

allocate provide hand over donate support ~~inherit~~ present cater leave sponsor hand down

Example Lisa .....inherited..... her flat from her parents.

1 The prisoners had to .... all their personal possessions to a prison officer.
2 A lot of people regularly........................... money to medical and other charities.
3 I would like to .... you with this clock in appreciation of your long service.
4 Jeff .... a lot of money by his grandfather.
5 Eva got a job to .... the family while her husband completed his degree.
6 The college has several cafés to .... for its students and staff.
7 I can .... you with all the pens and paper you need for the course.
8 This house has been .... through the generations of the Orford family.
9 I'm planning to run a marathon for charity and am asking all my friends to .... me.
10 As the students arrived at the hostel they were each .... a room.

55.4 **Choose the correct words in these sentences.**

7 marks

Example Patrick is now the *landlord / tenant /*(*proprietor*)of half a dozen corner shops.

1 Our school has been *supplied / allocated / presented* forty tickets for the concert.
2 If you move to a smaller flat, you may have to let *go / get / leave* of some of your possessions.
3 Jo's mother *catered / contributed / supported* her financially for six months while she was starting up her business.
4 Do you know how much money Greg *inherited / left / sponsored* when he died?
5 Did Patti's company *present / provide / cater* her with anything when she retired?
6 The most expensive *proprietors / belongings / properties* in the city are those next to the river.
7 I once had a summer job *handing over / giving out / letting go of* publicity flyers.

Your score

/35

56.1 Make sentences with the verbs and phrases in the table.

10 marks

subject	verb	sentence ending
~~The traffic~~	stir	at high speed along the new track.
1 The river	swayed	along the road towards school.
2 The car	drifted	~~slowly along the busy motorway.~~
3 The ferry	fluttered	in the light wind.
4 The train	travelled	to avoid a cat.
5 The clouds	drove	across the Channel.
6 The flag	~~moved~~	in the gentle breeze.
7 The leaves began to	flowed	away at high speed with two passengers in it.
8 The trees	dawdled	across the sky.
9 The lorry had to	sailed	through the valley.
10 The children	swerve	in the strong wind.

Example The traffic moved slowly along the busy motorway.

56.2 Put S for *slow* or F for *fast* next to each of these verbs. Then write the past simple form.

12 marks

verb	past simple
dawdle S	dawdled
hurry	
crawl	
tear	
shoot	
creep	
plod	

56.3 Complete these sentences with: *speed, rate, velocity* or *pace.*

6 marks

Example Both cars were travelling at ....speed......... when the accident happened.

1 This gun fires a high-............................... bullet which can penetrate metal.
2 The birth .... in Europe has decreased in the last thirty years.
3 Japan has some of the best high-............................... trains in the world.
4 The teacher went through the material at a very slow .... and the students got bored.
5 She could hear footsteps behind her so she quickened her ....
6 The drug has been shown to have a very high success ....

56.4 Choose the correct words in these sentences.

7 marks

Example The River Cam *travels / moves /*(*runs*) through Cambridge.

1 The train was travelling at a *rate / run / speed* of 100 kph.
2 Fewer ships *flow / sail / drive* across the Atlantic than in the past.
3 When are you planning to *run / change / move* to your new house?
4 We *plodded / rushed / shot* along the road, tired and laden with shopping.
5 The children *tore / travelled / fluttered* off down the road after the runaway puppy.
6 Come on, Billy. Stop *creeping / plodding / dawdling* – we'll miss our bus.
7 Look at that tree *hurrying / swaying / stirring* from side to side – I think it might fall.

Your score

/35

Texture, brightness, weight and density

57.1

10 marks

Match the words on the left with a suitable object on the right.

Example rough [f]

1 smooth ☐
2 sleek ☐
3 prickly ☐
4 shady ☐
5 slippery ☐
6 coarse ☐
7 jagged ☐
8 furry ☐
9 dazzling ☐
10 cumbersome ☐

a sunlight
b the corner of a garden
c a kitten
d heavy furniture
e a baby's skin
f the bark of a tree
g a cactus
h large grains of sand
i the exterior of a brand-new sports car
j a wet floor
k pieces of broken glass

57.2

10 marks

What are the correct words? (The first letters are given.)

Example What could you call well-polished leather shoes? s h i n y

1 What could you call part of a garden that doesn't get much light? s _ _ _ _
2 What could you call light that you can't see for a short time after looking at it? d _ _ _ _ _ _ _
3 What can you call a plant like a rose or a thistle that has sharp points sticking out of it?
  p _ _ _ _ _ _
4 What might you call furniture that takes up a lot of room? b _ _ _ _
5 What might you call hair that looks smooth, shiny and well-brushed? s _ _ _ _
6 What might you call mountains that are rough with sharp points? j _ _ _ _ _
7 How can you say that something is extremely light in weight? It's as light as a f _ _ _ _ _ _ .
8 How can you say that something is extremely heavy? It's as heavy as l _ _ _ .
9 How might you describe wooden furniture that you can see your reflection in?
  highly p _ _ _ _ _ _ _
10 How can you describe the trunk of a tree which is empty inside? h _ _ _ _ _

57.3

10 marks

Find the pairs of opposite adjectives. Then match each pair to the most appropriate noun.

Example rough / smooth skin

Adjectives

rough	dense	dull	fine	heavy	hollow
light	vivid	smooth	solid	sparse	thick

Nouns

bricks	colours	hair	skin	suitcase	vegetation

57.4

5 marks

Choose the correct words in these sentences.

Example The explorer had to cut his way through the *sparse /*(dense) jungle.

1 I love the *feel / touch* of fur on my skin.
2 Wear rubber boots because it will be very wet *underground / underfoot*.
3 There was black ice on the *top / surface* of the road and drivers were warned to take extra care.
4 This jumper is so lovely and soft to the *feel / touch*.
5 A deer was standing in the middle of the road in the *glare / shine* of the headlights.

Your score

/35

Success, failure and difficulty

58.1 Complete the table.

10 marks

verb	noun	adjective
accomplish	accomplishment	
succeed		
attain		
		hard
fulfil		
		difficult

58.2 Correct the mistakes in the underlined parts of these sentences.

8 marks

Example It was so noisy in the cafe <u>I had troubles understanding</u> what she was saying.
        I had trouble understanding

1 <u>We managed finishing</u> the project a year in advance.
2 I'll go running with you but I don't think <u>I can succeed ten kilometres</u>. Can we do five instead?
3 The company <u>has accomplished to do a great deal</u> this year.
4 I'm doubtful whether <u>her plans will come away,</u> but I hope they will for her sake.
5 The company has not <u>achieved to reach its targets</u> for the year.
6 I <u>succeeded to persuade</u> him to come with us.
7 Maggie <u>has been having considerable successes with</u> her research.
8 Terry <u>had many difficulties finding</u> a job.

58.3 Tick the possible collocations and put a ✗ next to the impossible ones.

12 marks

Example reach – an ambition ✗, a dream ✗, an agreement ✓, an obligation ✗, a target ✓,
        a compromise ✓

1 attain – an ambition, a dream, an agreement, an obligation, a target, a compromise
2 secure – an ambition, a dream, an agreement, an obligation, a target, a compromise
3 realise – an ambition, a dream, an agreement, an obligation, a target, a compromise
4 fulfil – an ambition, a dream, an agreement, an obligation, a target, a compromise
5 achieve – an ambition, a dream, an agreement, an obligation, a target, a compromise

58.4 Complete the sentences with the correct prepositions.

5 marks

Example I do hope Michelle's plans to arrange a class reunion will come ......off...... !

1 Josh's plans to take a gap year travelling round the world have come .... nothing as he just can't afford it at the moment.
2 I hope you will succeed .... everything you do.
3 It's hard for a mother to cope .... two children under the age of three.
4 The recession has hit businesses hard with a lot of smaller firms going .... in the last few months.
5 Ever since she fell, Grandma has had a lot of bother .... her knee.

Time: connecting words and expressions

59.1

10 marks

Correct the mistakes in these sentences.

Example A̶ moment I met him, I knew I'd marry him. *The*

1 She was flying into Paris in the very time that I was flying out.
2 I realised I'd left my keys on the kitchen table as just I closed the front door.
3 Prior taking up a position with Reynolds, Morris worked at CentreBank.
4 A new school library is currently under construction. During the meantime the children are using the City Library.
5 We'll deal with those issues on a later stage in the project.
6 I was home by midday but I had to go out earlier in.
7 Katy's moving to London in September but in the meanwhile she's living with us.
8 I'll have to repair the fence on some point but it's not too urgent.
9 Following of my holiday job in a hospital, I decided to train as a nurse.
10 I last saw Peter at Maria's wedding. In that occasion he was unusually friendly towards me.

59.2

9 marks

Put the words / phrases in the correct columns.

l̶a̶t̶e̶r̶ earlier on following formerly previously simultaneously thereafter subsequently the very moment prior

before	after	at the same time
	later	

59.3

8 marks

Explain the differences between these pairs of sentences.

Example a) Prior to my visit to France, I did some French courses.
b) Following my visit to France, I did some French courses.
In a) the speaker did the courses before the visit to France and in b) s/he did them after the visit.

1 a) My parents lived in Cambridge throughout the war.
b) My parents lived in Cambridge during the war.
2 a) Sally arrived at the very time I was leaving.
b) Sally arrived as I was leaving.
3 a) I wrote the novel and simultaneously thought about how it could be turned into a film script.
b) I wrote the novel and subsequently thought about how it could be turned into a film script.
4 a) The city was formerly known as Leningrad.
b) The city was subsequently known as Leningrad.

59.4

8 marks

Choose the correct words in these sentences.

Example The film starts at 8. What would you like to do before *this /* (*that*)?

1 I have no plans to leave here in the *immediate / simultaneous* future but eventually I'd like to work abroad.
2 We left the house *even / just* as the rain was starting.
3 *The / A* minute I opened the door, I knew this was the house I wanted to live in.
4 We had a great holiday in Spain. *Previously / Formerly* neither of us had ever spent more than a couple of days there.
5 Let's get together at *some / a* point *throughout / during* the holidays.
6 I studied Russian at university and went to Russia on many *occasions / times* in my twenties and thirties but rather less often *following / thereafter*.

Your score

/35

60 Condition

60.1
10 marks
Rewrite the sentences using the words in brackets.

Example If you don't mind carrying the bags, you can certainly come. (providing)
   Providing you don't mind carrying the bags, you can certainly come.

1 If there is a fire, use the staircase rather than the lift. (event)
2 Supposing you don't get the work finished on time; is that going to be a major problem? (what)
3 It doesn't matter when you get up tomorrow. (whenever)
4 You must have a visa to enter the country. (unless)
5 Take a warm coat with you as it might get cold in the evenings. (case)
6 Whatever happens, I'll always love you. (matter)
7 You can stay with us as long as you like provided that you help out with the housework. (condition)
8 There's no way I would agree to move house again. (circumstances)
9 It's going to take a long time to get there, no matter which route you take. (whichever)
10 You can join the tennis club providing you're over 16. (long)

60.2
10 marks
Find the mistakes in these sentences, then write correct versions.

Example He won't pass his exam unless he ~~will work~~ harder.
   He won't pass his exam unless he works harder.

1 Skype makes it easier to keep in touch with family whoever they are in the world.
2 Make sure you have your mobile phone with you in the case of an emergency.
3 What about we don't have enough money to pay for the meal, what'll happen then?
4 Take your driving licence with you in case you will decide to hire a car.
5 I wouldn't share a flat with her under no circumstances.

60.3
5 marks
Complete the sentences with the correct words. (The first letters are given.)

Example Take your scarf in c _a_ _s_ _e_ it's cold later on.

1 What are the entry r _ _ _ _ _ _ _ _ _ _ for a language course at your university?
2 Grants are available for students who meet certain c _ _ _ _ _ _ _ _ _ .
3 I wouldn't agree to those terms under any c _ _ _ _ _ _ _ _ _ _ _ _ .
4 In the e _ _ _ _ of a strike, the army will take over some of the responsibilities of the police.
5 Having a clean driving licence is a p _ _ _ _ _ _ _ _ _ _ _ for the job.

60.4
10 marks
Choose the correct words in these sentences.

Example How / (What) if no one's there to meet me?

1 I just can't understand algebra no matter *how / very* hard I try.
2 *Supposed / Supposing* you're right and there's a problem with the budget, what should we do about it?
3 You can go to your dad's office today *so / such* long as you don't get in the way.
4 I'll help you today on condition *when / that* you help me next week.
5 *Under / Over* what circumstances would you consider resigning from your job?
6 You can't park here *if / unless* you don't have a special permit.
7 I'll buy you a bike *on / in* condition that you always wear a cycle helmet.
8 *Whenever / Whoever* Tanya decides to marry, he won't be considered good enough by her dad.
9 Take some ID just in *case / event* they ask for it.
10 Passing a written test on the Highway Code, is a *circumstance / prerequisite* for taking the practical driving test.

Your score

/35

61.1 Complete the sentences with the correct prepositions.

10 marks

Example They bought the flat with a view ......*to*...... renting it out to students.

1 Recent photos have given rise .... speculation that the princess may be expecting a baby.
2 Eventually, anger about the degree of social inequality in the country brought .... a revolution.
3 Liang's enthusiasm for wildlife photography stems .... his childhood interest in observing birds in his garden.
4 The course has been cancelled owing .... a shortage of suitable applicants.
5 Today's lecture is going to be on the causes .... the First World War.
6 What do you think is the reason .... Mel's decision to leave the company?
7 Pavel wrote his article with the aim .... persuading others to accept his point of view.
8 Sonya worked hard and, ... a consequence, did very well in her exams.
9 Simon was sacked from his job .... the grounds that he had given confidential information to a competitor.
10 Last year's floods resulted .... many insurance claims.

61.2 Put the words in the correct columns.

7 marks

~~aim~~ consequence motive grounds outcome purpose upshot reason

used to explain why something happened	used to give the result of something that happened
aim	

61.3 Rewrite the sentences using the words in brackets.

10 marks

Example We couldn't agree terms and consequently the deal fell through. (consequence)
   We couldn't agree terms and as a consequence the deal fell through.

1 The editor knew the article would give rise to a lot of comment. (spark)
2 The shopping mall will provide local people with a range of jobs. (generate)
3 There was thick fog and so our plane couldn't take off. (owing)
4 What made Cathy change her mind about handing in her notice? (caused)
5 Our problems are the result of a misunderstanding. (stem)
6 Why was Smith not at today's meeting? (reason)
7 The teacher explained to the class why they were doing the activity. (purpose)
8 I never heard how the discussions ended. (upshot)
9 The police are trying to discover why Briggs stole the file. (motive)
10 I suspect the Minister's speech will lead to an angry response. (prompt)

61.4 Correct the mistakes in these sentences.

8 marks

Example The accident was caused ~~for~~ a deer running across the road. *by*

1 Owing to the weather was bad, the open air concert was cancelled.
2 I think her charm is the reason of Juliet's success.
3 First, we have to deal with some matters raising from the last meeting.
4 Tim's talk promoted a heated argument.
5 I left my purse at home and, subsequently, had to walk back rather than get a bus.
6 We left the door open and, for a result, the rain came in and soaked the carpet.
7 Let me start by explaining the purpose from this project.
8 The match resulted to a draw.

Your score

/35

62.1 Choose the correct option in these sentences.

10 marks

Example It's a convenient place to live. (On the other hand)/ *On the contrary* it's very expensive.

1 I *permit / accept* that you worked hard but your assignment simply isn't good enough.
2 I *reverse / concede* you're right on some counts but certainly not on all.
3 Bella is a keen musician. Her twin, *in contrast / on the contrary*, is more focused on sport.
4 *Although / Nevertheless* she has the right build for a ballet dancer, she doesn't have the determination.
5 I'm afraid our positions on this issue are *a yawning gap / poles apart*.
6 *Admittedly / Agreeably*, he means well but he has created a lot of problems for the company.
7 I know he's only trying to help us. *That's all very well / On the other hand* but he should have spoken to us first.
8 The President has *acknowledged / conceded* his own involvement in the affair.
9 There's *poles apart / a huge discrepancy* between the two witnesses' testimonies.
10 I thought Oxford would beat Cambridge. In fact, *there's a yawning gap / the reverse was true*.

62.2 Complete the sentences with the correct words. (The first letters are given.)

14 marks

Example There's a y a w n i n g g a p between what he says and what he does.

1 It's a _ _ v _ _ _ w _ _ _ apologising but you must also pay for the damage you caused.
2 At first I thought he was stupid but in fact the r _ _ _ _ _ _ is t _ _ _ – he's extremely intelligent.
3 It's a very expensive trip but o _ the o _ _ _ _ h _ _ _ it's the only chance we're likely to get to go there.
4 There's no point getting the TV repaired. A _ _ _ _ a _ _, we're getting a new one next month.
5 There's a w _ _ _ _ of d _ _ _ _ _ _ _ _ _ between something being difficult and something being impossible.
6 He's lazy and rude but, for a _ _ t _ _ _, he's an old friend and I want to help him.

62.3 Rewrite the sentences using the words in brackets.

4 marks

Example He's fun and friendly but, despite that, he's not right for the job. (for)
He's fun and friendly but, for all that, he's not right for the job.

1 Admittedly, it's an interesting plan but it simply isn't practical. (concede)
2 The flat is pleasantly spacious but, against that, it'd need a lot of decorating. (hand)
3 There's a yawning gap between the two parties' environmental policies. (poles)
4 At that time, the lifestyles of the urban and rural classes were totally different. (divide)

62.4 Match the beginning of each phrase with its ending.

7 marks

Example for all that

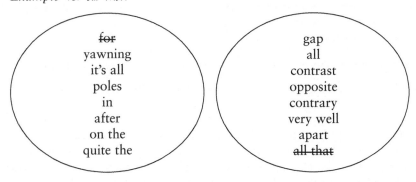

~~for~~	gap
yawning	all
it's all	contrast
poles	opposite
in	contrary
after	very well
on the	apart
quite the	~~all that~~

Your score
/35

63.1
10 marks

Complete the sentences with the correct prepositions.

Example I'm writing a book on Soviet education: schools, universities, colleges and so ....on.... .

1 It's going to be a very busy summer what with Sam's graduation, three family weddings and, ... top .... all that, Grandma's 80th birthday party.
2 We should take our swimming things and a ball to the beach along .... a picnic.
3 Further .... our letter of 18 June, we now enclose an application form.
4 Hannah's lovely – kind, friendly and intelligent .... the bargain.
5 We've got to read page 5 at home .... addition .... the work we were given yesterday.
6 The CEO came to the meeting together .... one or two other people from Head Office.
7 Apart .... the stormy weather, did you enjoy the holiday?
8 .... well as being a keen swimmer, Urs does a lot of horse-riding too.

63.2
10 marks

Rewrite the sentences using the words in brackets.

Example He has a van as well as a family car. (besides) *Besides having a family car, he has a van.*

1 He's very good-looking and he's a nice person too. (more)
2 I help out with the housework and also do some cooking. (addition)
3 Jon can be very bad-tempered, but, to be fair, his wife also has a very sharp tongue. (equally)
4 They sell food, clothes, electrical goods, etc. (forth)
5 Following your letter of 6 May, I am sending you the information you require. (further)
6 It was cold and dark and, to make things worse, the baby was screaming. (top)
7 Staff in this job need a knowledge of languages and a driving licence too. (additionally)
8 Luke's a brilliant mathematician and a talented singer into the bargain. (boot)
9 Jennie came to the rehearsal accompanied by two of her friends. (along)
10 Your tennis would benefit from both specialist coaching and more practice. (as well as)

63.3
8 marks

Correct the mistakes in these sentences.

Example Further ~~on~~ our recent phone call, the furniture will be delivered next Monday. *to*

1 Alongside with her own job, she also helps out her husband with his business.
2 Besides they have a flat in London, they also own a cottage in the country.
3 We've got to paint the kitchen this weekend and tidy the garden for boot.
4 In addition to he speaks Russian, Tim knows a bit of Korean.
5 It's an interesting old town. Furthermoreover, it has a world-class university.
6 I feed the cats once a day, or likewise the dog.
7 We had to fill in a form, then have an interview, and so forth and so on.
8 I need to get my passport renewed and plus I need to have some inoculations done.

63.4
7 marks

Complete the sentences with the expressions from the box.

| likewise   plus   and so on and so forth   into the bargain |
| ~~alongside~~   further to   apart from   on top of all that |

Example It will be very hard work to do a degree ....*alongside*.......... a full-time job.

1 It's hard enough cooking for Clare's family as it is, as her children are very fussy about their food but, ... , her husband is allergic to eggs.
2 .... your phone call, I am sending you the information you requested.
3 The house is light, spacious, not too expensive and well-decorated ....
4 I can't go out this evening. I've got a lot of work to do, ... I can't afford it.
5 .... his work at the hotel, Julian spends a lot of time playing the piano for a singer.
6 Before we go away, I need to sort out my clothes, get my suit dry-cleaned, arrange for the dog to go into kennels ....
7 Liam's parents are pleased with his progress this term. .... his teachers.

Your score

/35

64.1 Put the words in the correct groups.

10 marks

~~approach~~ answer assessment attitude crisis difficulty
judgement key position reaction state of affairs

situation	
problem	
response	approach
solution	
evaluation	

64.2 Complete the sentences with the correct prepositions.

10 marks

Example There is no easy answer ....to......... the question.

1 What would you say could be the solution .... the problem?
2 It's hard to see a way .... the situation.
3 What was Hiroshi's parents' reaction .... his decision?
4 Our position .... regard .... contracts has not changed.
5 Our evaluation .... the government's approach is outlined below.
6 A knowledge of history is key .... understanding the current situation.
7 The economic state .... affairs is causing some concern.
8 The attitude .... university education has changed over recent years.

64.3 Complete the sentences with the words from the box.

5 marks

aspect point ~~affect~~ argument matters question

Example I don't think the rail strike will ....affect....... this area too badly.

1 I don't understand the .... that George is trying to make, do you?
2 The government's approach to the problem actually seems to be making .... worse.
3 Will the President resign or won't he is the .... that is intriguing journalists at the moment.
4 The cost of recycling waste is just one .... of the problem.
5 The fact that even trivial incidents can have extraordinary consequences is the central .... of the book.

64.4 Choose the better word to describe each sentence.

10 marks

Example The problem is becoming more serious. *(A view)* or *a way out?*

1 Without oxygen people cannot live. *A fact* or *a claim?*
2 Why should I do it? Why can't someone else do it? *A reaction* or *a matter?*
3 Love can overcome any difficulties in life. *A dilemma* or *a claim?*
4 The law will be changed to close up existing loopholes. *A problem* or *a solution?*
5 The purpose of art. *A topic* or *a key?*
6 Babies should be fed at regular times rather than on demand. *A crisis* or *an approach?*
7 It's time for a change of government. *An assessment* or *a difficulty?*
8 The polar ice caps are melting. *An attitude* or *an issue?*
9 Rioting in inner cities. *A judgement* or *a state of affairs?*
10 Reducing poverty would also reduce crime. *An argument* or *a dilemma?*

Your score

/35

Discourse markers in spoken English

65.1

10 marks

Choose the best options in these dialogues.

Example A: I'm sorry I missed Paul yesterday.

   B: Yes, *sort of / great /* (*still*) you'll see him next week.

1 A: She's always annoying me. B: *Fine / Well then / I mean*, you should tell her.
2 A: I just don't know what to do. B: *Sort of / Listen / You know*, I've got an idea.
3 A: What's the matter? B: It's oh, *right / you know / anyway*, the same old problem.
4 A: They'll be here at about 5.30. B: *Fine / Hold on / Still*, I'll be here waiting for them.
5 A: Here's a package for you. B: *Right / You know / Sort of*, leave it on the desk.
6 A: What happened? B: Josie, *so / listen / I mean*, Julie, forgot to buy tickets.
7 A: What do you mean, he's unfriendly? B: Well, *still / for instance / fine*, he never smiles at you.
8 A: What's the matter with you? B: Guess I'm *hold on / sort of / now then* worried about the test.
9 A: Why not come with us? B: Well, **a**, you're leaving too early and *so / well then / **b*** the car's too small.
10 A: Could you give me Jack's email? B: Sure, *fine / hold on / anyway*, let me just check what it is.

65.2

5 marks

Match the words in Box A with the words in Box B.

Example I mean

Box A | I hang now you well mind

Box B | see you ~~mean~~ on then then

65.3

20 marks

Complete the missing phrase in each sentence. (The first letters are given, except for number 10.) Then match each phrase with the relevant comment on its use (a–k).

Example N o w t h e n, I'd like you all to turn to page 15. h

1 M _ _ _ y _ _, it's already 6.30, so she's probably not coming.
2 L _ _ _, why don't you let me pay for this now?
3 W _ _ _ _ w _ _ I? Oh, yes, I'd just looked at my watch when ...
4 Her address? L _ _ m _ s _ _, it's in my address book, I think.
5 I think this is what we have to do. A _ _ _ _ _, there'll be time to check tomorrow.
6 Galina was wearing these, l _ _ _, riding boots. She looked amazing.
7 H _ _ _ o _, let me tell you what he actually said.
8 I don't earn a huge amount. S _ _ _ _, it's enough to live on.
9 She's a bit difficult sometimes. I m _ _ _, she can be rather moody.
10 Well, _, I can't afford it and, _, I haven't got the time to go there either.

a used when you're not sure how to say something
b used to introduce a suggestion or important point
c used to list points
d used to gain time to think or do something
e used to make a contrast between two points
f used to introduce an afterthought
g used to prevent an interruption
h used by the person in charge of the conversation to introduce an instruction
i used before an explanation of what you're trying to say
j used to suggest that the topic can now change, there's nothing more to be said
k used after an interruption to come back to the main topic or story

Your score
/35

66.1 **Write linking words / phrases to replace the words in brackets. (The first letters are given.)**

10 marks

Example (As a last point), let us consider the effect on the environment. F̲i̲n̲a̲l̲l̲y̲...

1 (Changing the subject to) the question of the effects of violence on TV, the evidence is inconclusive. T............................ t..............

2 (To draw the argument to a close), we may say that the advantages outweigh the disadvantages. I.............. c............................

3 (Put in a very short way), there are two objections to the plan. B..............

4 (As point number two), employees need to feel valued. S............................

5 (To repeat what has already been said more concisely), the project has proved very successful. T.............. s.............. u..............

6 (To continue), let us now consider the case of foster children. N..............

7 (As point number three), let us consider the history of the region. T..............

8 (While not discussing any further) the issue of childcare, let us now consider work opportunities for single parents. L............................ a............................

9 (As a side comment), there was a similar case in 1949. I.............. p............................

10 (The first point is), we should not be swayed by personal feelings. F..............

66.2 **Find pairs with similar meanings.**

6 marks

Example first of all – firstly

(as it were) (finally) (~~first of all~~) (in summary)

(~~firstly~~)

(for instance) (in conclusion) (in other words) (that is to say)

(so to speak)

(lastly) (say) (to conclude) (to sum up)

66.3 **Read the statements and tick True or False.**

11 marks

	True	False
Example In parenthesis is used to draw attention to a key point.	☐	✓
1 *For example* means exactly the same as *For instance*.	☐	☐
2 *That is to say* means the same as *in other words* but is less formal.	☐	☐
3 The preposition that follows *with reference* is *for*.	☐	☐
4 *It was stated over* can be used instead of *It was stated earlier* to refer to something written in a previous part of the text.	☐	☐
5 *Overleaf* means *on the opposite page*.	☐	☐
6 *For further information* is used to mean the same as *For more information*.	☐	☐
7 *So to speak* means the same as, but is more formal than, *As it were*.	☐	☐
8 *In sum* is more formal than *In summary* or *To sum up*.	☐	☐
9 *The table underneath* is used to mean the same as *The following table*.	☐	☐
10 An academic writer is more likely to say *Look at the tables in the appendix* than *See the tables in the appendix*.	☐	☐
11 *First of all* can also be written as one word.	☐	☐

66.4 **Now correct the False statements in 66.3.**

8 marks

Example 'In parenthesis' is used to mention something in passing.

(Your score)

/35

67.1 Put the words in the correct order to make expressions.

10 marks

Example say you as   *as you say*

1 you if me ask
2 saying I as was
3 it to come of think
4 else if fails all
5 thing with what and another one

6 luck it would as have
7 I'm as concerned as far
8 reminds that me
9 worst the if to worst the comes
10 that and other the this

67.2 Match the bold phrases in sentences 1–10 with explanations a–k.

10 marks

Example **As luck would have it**, I bumped into Andrew at the station.   `9`

1 **Talking of** engineers, how's that cousin of yours in Africa?   ☐

2 **That reminds me**, I haven't paid the phone bill yet.   ☐

3 **If you ask me**, it's complete rubbish.   ☐

4 **If all else fails**, call me on this number.   ☐

5 **If the worst comes to the worst**, we'll have to cancel the meeting.   ☐

6 **What with one thing and another**, I haven't managed to finish the report.   ☐

7 **When it comes to** opera singers, Pamparoni is the best in the world, in my opinion.

8 **Come to think of it**, Lars still hasn't been in touch. I wonder what's happening.

9 **As you say**, it won't happen before July.   ☐

10 **As I was saying**, we'll need to get up early tomorrow.   ☐

a something in the conversation makes you remember something important
b repeats and confirms something someone else has already said
c if the situation gets very bad and there is no alternative
d if you've tried everything but are not successful
e because of a lot of different circumstances
f starting a new topic but linking to the previous one
g by a fortunate chance
h takes the conversation back to an earlier point
i if you want my opinion (even if no one has asked for it)
j something in the conversation makes you realise there may be a problem / query about something
k if it is a question of / if we are talking about

67.3 Complete the sentences with *this* or *that*.

6 marks

Example We had a lovely evening talking about ....*this*........ , that and the other.

1 A: I've agreed to take the job. B: So that's .... , then?
2 A: What did you talk about then? B: Nothing much, just .... and ....
3 .... reminds me. I must ring Grandma.
4 A: Have you got any more money for me? B: No .... 's it, I'm afraid.
5 A: They don't pay us very well here, do they? B: Well, ... is it. I'm finding it really hard.

67.4 Complete the sentences with the correct words.

9 marks

Example: ....*As*............ I was saying, it's not the best time to be looking for work.

1 As .... as I'm .... , both of the flats we looked at are equally convenient.
2 When it .... to railway history, Mike's the man you need.
3 As luck would .... it, Maria had the papers we needed in her bag.
4 If .... else .... , we could always take a taxi to the restaurant.
5 What .... one thing and .... , my hair appointment completely slipped my mind.
6 If you .... me, there are problems ahead.

 Your score

/35

68 Talking and communicating

68.1
10 marks

Complete the sentences with the phrases from the box.

> ball rolling   get to the point   long-winded   put it in a nutshell   rubbish
> sense   small talk   speak her mind   talk down   talk shop   ~~talking to~~

Example I need to give Jamie a ....*talking to*.... . His room is in a terrible mess.

1 That lecturer is so .... – it takes him ages to ....
2 Please stop discussing work. I hate it when people .... at parties.
3 You can't believe anything he says. He usually talks utter .... His wife on the
   other hand can sometimes talk a lot of .... I rather like the way she tends to
   .... , saying exactly what she thinks.
4 To .... , the conference was a success from start to finish.
5 There was only time for a few minutes of .... before we had to get down
   to business.
6 Karen started the .... by suggesting a few questions for us to discuss in pairs.
7 Viktor has a terrible tendency to .... to other people, as if he thinks they are
   less intelligent than he is.

68.2
5 marks

Choose the best explanations for the sentences.

Example Don't talk such rubbish!
> *Don't talk about the environment /* (Don't say silly things) */ Don't be so cross!*

1 Reema couldn't make head or tail of what James was telling her.
   Reema *could not hear / could not understand / could not agree with* James.
2 They were talking at cross purposes.
   They were *talking angrily / about two different things / with the same intention.*
3 Marta got the wrong end of the stick.
   Marta *took something by mistake / misunderstood / was unfairly accused.*
4 It's hard to get a word in edgeways with her.
   It's hard *to convince her / to say something because she talks so much / to criticise her.*
5 It's not good to talk about someone behind their back.
   It's not good *to criticise someone in their absence / to comment on someone's appearance / to
   speak negatively of someone in a public place.*

68.3
16 marks

Find the mistakes in these sentences then write correct versions.

Example ~~Talking~~ your mind can sometimes get you into trouble.
> *Speaking your mind can sometimes get you into trouble.*

1 I think it's time to wrap off the discussions, don't you?
2 The actor never imagined the film would become such a speaking point.
3 You can never get a word in sideways when Barry's around.
4 I'm afraid Megan's husband is not much good at little talk.
5 So, who'd like to start the ball moving?
6 To put it in a nut, the whole evening was a disaster.
7 Dad is inclined to get the wrong end of the pole.
8 I can't make heads or tails of Richard's book.

68.4
4 marks

Match the statements with the appropriate responses.

Example A: Mark needs a good talking to.   B: Yes, he loves the sound of his own voice.
1 A: Joe won't have much time for his speech.   B: Yes, he'll need to get to the point quickly.
2 A: Dan can be patronising, can't he?   B: Yes, he does tend to talk down to people.
3 A: I wish Andrei weren't so long-winded.   B: Yes, it's time he got down to work.
4 A: You can rely on Ramzi to talk sense.   B: Yes, he knows what he's talking about.

Your score

/35

69.1
10 marks

Make words ending in *-er* / *-or* with each of these roots.

Example act ....*actor*........

1 sail ....
2 sharpen ....
3 operate ....
4 shop ....
5 project ....
6 employ ....
7 supervise ....
8 hang ....
9 grate ....
10 donate ....

69.2
10 marks

Make the nouns from these verbs / adjectives.

Example flexible .....*flexibility*....

1 excite ....
2 pollute ....
3 ready ....
4 admit ....
5 scarce ....
6 forgetful ....
7 replace ....
8 complicate ....
9 reduce ....
10 happy ....

69.3
5 marks

What do we call ...

Example ... a person who believes in the ideas of Karl Marx? *a Marxist*

1 .... a person who plays the piano? ....
2 .... a person to whom a letter is addressed? ....
3 .... a person who studies physics? ....
4 .... a person who is employed by someone? ....
5 .... a person who plays the cello? ....

69.4
10 marks

Complete the sentences with words formed from the words in brackets.

Example Don't worry – the water here is perfectly ....*drinkable*......... . (drink)

1 We've moved into a lovely old house but we'll have to .... the kitchen. (modern)
2 It always takes me a long time in the morning to .... myself! (beauty)
3 The government's .... to listen to what ordinary people are saying may cost them the election. (refuse)
4 Anna finds .... the most fulfilling side of her life. (mother)
5 I thought the teenagers' behaviour in court was absolutely .... (outrage)
6 Don't be afraid of that spider – it's totally .... (harm)
7 I really value your .... – it means a great deal to me. (friend)
8 *Wrote* is an .... form of the verb and *was written* is passive. (act)
9 I thought Oscar's treatment of his girlfriend was .... and do not understand why she put up with it for so long. (forgive)
10 Nothing could spoil my .... of the play. (enjoy)

Your score
/35

70.1 Add a prefix to one word from each A sentence in order to make an opposite word to
10 marks complete each B response.

Example A: He's quite mature for his age.   B: I don't agree I think he's very ....*immature*...... .

1 A: Is it legal to drive so fast here?   B: No, it's ....
2 A: Is she wrapping that parcel?   B: No, she's .... it.
3 A: Is his handwriting legible?   B: No, I find it quite ....
4 A: Does her father approve of Joe?   B: No, he .... of him.
5 A: Do you think he's an experienced skier?   B: No, I know he's ....
6 A: Would you say she's a patient person?   B: No, she's very ....
7 A: Can I replace the vase I broke?   B: No, I'm afraid it's ....
8 A: Do you like your boss?   B: No, I .... him intensely.
9 A: Are these mushrooms edible?   B: No, I'm pretty sure they're ....
10 A: That man's locking the door.   B: No, he isn't. He's .... it.

70.2 Match the prefixes on the left with the correct meanings on the right.
11 marks

Example anti *against*

1 auto-   a after
2 bi-   b small
3 ex-   c many
4 ex-   d under
5 in-   e one
6 in-   f two
7 micro-   g not
8 mono-   h into
9 multi-   i former
10 post-   j of or by oneself
11 sub-   k out of

70.3 Use your knowledge of prefixes to explain these words / phrases.
10 marks

Example a pseudo-intellectual .... *someone who pretends to be intellectual but isn't really* ....

1 an ex-soldier ....
2 to be semi-literate ....
3 to reread ....
4 to misspell ....
5 to be pro-army ....
6 to overemphasise ....
7 to undervalue ....
8 to be anti-government ....
9 a subconscious act ....
10 pre-wedding ....

70.4 Which is the odd one out? Explain why.
4 marks

Example internal, insert, income, (indiscreet)
             In 'indiscreet', 'in' means 'not'; in the other words 'in' means 'into'.

1 disconnect, disappear, dissimilar, disbelieve
2 extract, ex-boss, exhale, excommunicate
3 unbend, unnatural, unfair, unconvincing
4 relevant, moral, sensitive, literate (Think about the opposite forms!)

71.1
10 marks

Replace the underlined words in these sentences with more formal equivalents formed from the roots in brackets.

Example We hired a van to ~~move~~ ....transport.... our furniture to the new flat. (PORT)

1 We all have rights but it's important to <u>think of</u> .... others' rights too. (SPECT)
2 Many politicians were <u>taught</u> .... at Oxford University. (DUCT)
3 This poem <u>says</u> .... exactly how autumn makes me feel. (PRESS)
4 My ancestors first came to Australia to <u>look</u> .... for gold. (SPECT)
5 This website quickly <u>changes</u> .... pounds into kilos and vice versa. (VERT)
6 The government has <u>put</u> .... a ban on the import of tobacco. (POSE)
7 Tina's father told her he could not <u>back up</u> .... her decision. (PORT)
8 The company <u>made</u> .... more cars this year than it did last year. (DUCT)
9 I tried going to work by a different route but soon <u>went back</u> .... to the old one. (VERT)
10 We were all very <u>struck</u> .... by the children's performances. (PRESS)

71.2
5 marks

Match the Latin roots on the left with their meanings on the right.

PRESS   place, put
DUCT   see, look
PONE, POSE press, push
PORT   turn
SPECT   carry, take
VERT   lead

71.3
10 marks

Write a word made from one of the roots in 71.2 to match each definition.

Example to look up to, to admire ...to respect...

1 to bring products into a country from another country ....
2 to direct the musicians in an orchestra ....
3 to put a monarch off their throne ....
4 to make you feel gloomy ....
5 to put off to a later date ....
6 to send traffic in a different direction ....
7 to expel a foreigner from a country ....
8 to check something carefully ....
9 to put money into a bank account ....
10 to change something into a different form ....

71.4
10 marks

Complete the table.

verb	person noun	abstract noun
educate	educator	education
inspect		
oppress		
compose		
advertise		
deport		

Abstract nouns

72.1
10 marks

Make an abstract noun from each of these words.

Example martyr ...*martyrdom*...

1 mother ....
2 disagree ....
3 apprentice ....
4 polite ....
5 reduce ....
6 wise ....
7 warm ....
8 friendly ....
9 popular ....
10 combine ....

72.2
12 marks

Complete the sentences with nouns formed from the words in brackets.

Example His face was so red with ....*anger*........... I thought he would have a heart attack there and then. (angry)

1 Vikram has a rather difficult .... with his father. (relate)
2 His writing shows a great deal of .... (sensitive)
3 Nicola is very much looking forward to her .... (retire)
4 Omar has always shown great .... to me. (kind)
5 There is considerable room for .... in your work. (improve)
6 The holiday certainly lived up to all our .... (expect)
7 My parents live in a quiet .... on the edge of town. (neighbour)
8 The actor said that .... is less enjoyable than many people think. (star)
9 The aim of the exhibition is to celebrate the college's many .... (achieve)
10 Most scientists tend to have a natural .... (curious)
11 Ayesha has been offered a .... in a top legal firm. (partner)
12 The government says that it believes in the .... of information. (free)

72.3
13 marks

Write the abstract noun forms of the words in the box under the correct headings in the table. Some of the words in the box are already in the correct form; others will need the correct suffix.

~~faith~~ bored calm careless companion affectionate fear frustrate generous hostile humorous lazy lucky rage

pleasant	unpleasant
faith	

Your score
/35

73.1 **Complete the compound adjectives with words from the box.**

10 marks

| absent | ~~curly~~ | free | hand | out | proof | so | top | two | world | up |

Example a ......*curly*...... -haired baby

1 .... -secret information
2 an .... -minded professor
3 a sugar-...................... diet
4 a .... -famous orchestra
5 a bullet-...................... jacket

6 a .... -faced hypocrite
7 .... -made jewellery
8 .... -called experts
9 hard-...................... students
10 worn-...................... slippers

73.2 **Match the collocations.**

10 marks

Example hard-working students

~~hard-working~~
air-conditioned
first-hand
open-necked
all-out
cut-price
long-standing
long-distance
well-off
built-up
off-peak

goods
relationship
areas
middle classes
~~students~~
knowledge
strike
shirt
travel
runner
rooms

73.3 **Rewrite each phrase using a compound adjective + a noun.**

7 marks

Example a child with rosy cheeks .... *a rosy-cheeked child* ....

1 shoes with open toes ....
2 a person with a big head ....
3 a skirt that fits tightly ....
4 a girl with a suntan ....
5 a job that consumes a lot of time ....
6 a man with broad shoulders ....
7 a loan that is free of interest ....

73.4 **Read the definitions and tick True or False. Correct the false definitions.**

8 marks

	True	False
Example an off-peak train ticket – a ticket for use in the rush hour	☐	✓
a ticket for use outside the rush hour		
1 a run-down area of town is a district that is poor and not well cared for	☐	☐
2 a brand-new car is one that is revolutionary in design	☐	☐
3 a duty-free shop is one where you can buy things without paying tax	☐	☐
4 a self-centred person is someone who is very kind and considerate	☐	☐
5 a stuck-up person is someone who is snobbish	☐	☐
6 a bad-tempered person is someone who is unattractive to look at	☐	☐
7 a full-time job is one where you have to work evenings and weekends	☐	☐
8 a first-born child is the oldest child in the family	☐	☐

Your score

/35

Compound nouns 1: noun + noun

74.1
10 marks
Pair the words to make ten compound nouns.

Example earring

(~~ear~~) (mark) (~~ring~~) (bag) (mineral) (fever)
(gap) (generation) (hay) (trade) (holiday) (hostel)
(money) (mother) (package) (water) (pocket)
(wool) (tea) (tongue) (cotton) (youth)

74.2
5 marks
Write a noun that can complete two compound nouns.

Example voice ......*mail*...... ; ......*mail*...... order

1 .... donor; .... pressure
2 .... clock; burglar ....
3 birth .... ; air traffic ....
4 junk .... ; .... poisoning
5 arms .... ; .... relations

74.3
8 marks
Complete the text with the correct compound nouns.

Sam is an elderly businessman. He had a heart ....*attack*.... last week while he was standing at
a (1) bus .... He had been upset by a letter telling him that his (2) bank ....
was overdrawn and by newspaper articles which he had read that morning about government
plans to reinstate the (3) death ...., to abolish the (4) welfare ...., to ignore the
problems of (5) climate .... and to increase (6) income .... The ambulance
went so fast it almost broke the (7) sound .... It also nearly had an accident as its
(8) windscreen .... were not working and it was raining heavily. Fortunately, it got
to the hospital safely and Sam has now fully recovered.

74.4
12 marks
Match these compound nouns to their definitions.

Definitions

Example a credit card [q]

1 a babysitter [ ]
2 grass roots [ ]
3 roadworks [ ]
4 traffic lights [ ]
5 a steering wheel [ ]
6 a pedestrian crossing [ ]
7 a tin opener [ ]
8 a human being [ ]
9 sunglasses [ ]
10 luxury goods [ ]
11 headphones [ ]
12 a contact lens [ ]

a a safe place for people to get to the other side of
  the road
b expensive products such as supercars or designer
  clothes
c repairs to, e.g. a street or motorway
d someone who looks after a child while its parents
  are out
e something you wear in your eye to help you see better
f the ordinary people in a society or organisation
g ~~a piece of plastic that can be used to pay for things~~
h things that control cars and other vehicles so they are
  not all trying to cross a junction at the same time
i things that help you see when it is a very bright day
j an implement that allows you to get food out of a can
k what a car driver holds when driving
l you wear these to listen to music so that others do
  not have to hear it too
m a person

Your score
/35

Compound nouns 2: verb + preposition

75.1 Match the compound nouns on the left with their meanings on the right.

10 marks

Example bypass ☐ e

1	breakthrough ☐	a	prospect
2	checkout ☐	b	reduction
3	crackdown ☐	c	strike
4	cutback ☐	d	major change
5	drawback ☐	e	road avoiding a town
6	outlook ☐	f	cash desk
7	shake-up ☐	g	money passing through a company
8	takeover ☐	h	disadvantage
9	turnover ☐	i	important discovery
10	walkout ☐	j	purchase of one company by another one
		k	action to prevent something

75.2 Complete the compound nouns with the correct prepositions.

10 marks

Example You must pay for your shopping at the check ....*out*.... .

1 After his lecture on nuclear fall .... , the professor gave the students a hand ....
2 The main draw .... of the new set-.............. is that there is a lot more paperwork.
3 The .... come of the customer feed .... survey was improved service.
4 Rapid staff turn .... this year has resulted in a reduction in .... put at the factory.
5 Nick blames his becoming a drop .... on the break-.............. of his parents' marriage.

75.3 Complete each second sentence with a noun based on the phrasal verb in the first.

10 marks

Example I'll print you out a copy of the figures. I'll give you a ......*printout*...... of the figures.

1 Yasmin works out daily at the gym. *Yasmin does daily .... at the gym.*
2 Modern bosses usually ask workers to feed back on new initiatives.
   Modern bosses usually ask workers for .... on new initiatives.
3 Conor was there when war broke out. *Conor was there at the .... of war.*
4 What you get out of a computer depends on what you put in.
   What you get out of a computer depends on your ....
5 The boss announced that he was cutting back our budget substantially.
   The boss announced that he was making substantial .... to our budget.
6 Talks broke down last night. *There was a .... in talks last night.*
7 Increasing numbers of people are dropping out from society.
   There are increasing numbers of .... in society.
8 Our company is planning to take over a major competitor next year.
   Our company is planning the .... of a major competitor next year.
9 I can print out our latest sales figures for you.
   I can give you a .... of our latest sales figures.
10 It didn't surprise me when their marriage broke up.
   The .... of their marriage didn't surprise me.

75.4 Choose the correct words in these sentences.

5 marks

Example I'd rather look at a *workout* / (*printout*) than figures on screen.

1 We stopped in a *lay-by* / *by-pass* to take some photos of the view over the valley.
2 It was clear from the *outcome* / *outset* that the project was unlikely to succeed.
3 This year the company has opened a number of new retail *outlets* / *set-ups*.
4 There has been a significant *breakdown* / *breakthrough* in the search for a cure for cancer.
5 The company's *takeover* / *turnover* is large but its profits are not enormous.

Your score

/35

76.1
10 marks
Make binomials by joining words from Box A to words from box B.

Example high and dry

| A | ~~high~~ | give | prim | rant | rough | wine | part | odds | rack | leaps | pick |

| B | ruin | choose | ends | dine | bounds | ~~dry~~ | ready | rave | take | parcel | proper |

76.2
10 marks
Complete the sentences with the binomials from 76.1.

Example Karl pulled out of the play at the last moment leaving the rest of the cast .... high and dry ....

1 The hotel was a bit .... but it was cheap and convenient.
2 The new boss is very .... The old one was more informal and easy-going.
3 The secret of a successful marriage is .... – being able to compromise.
4 He was furious and started to .... at us.
5 My English has progressed by .... during the course.
6 Hard work is .... of learning a language. There's no other way.
7 My friends in New York always .... me at the best restaurants.
8 The old house has gone to .... now. I can't afford to restore it.
9 It's a good course. You can .... from a range of interesting modules.
10 There are lots of .... to discuss before we finish the meeting but nothing major.

76.3
5 marks
Complete these binomials with *but, to* or *or*.

Example sink ......or...... swim

1 take it .... leave it
2 slowly .... surely
3 sooner .... later
4 all .... nothing
5 back .... front

76.4
10 marks
Complete the binomial expressions in the sentences. (The first letters are given.)

Example First and f o r e m o s t let me introduce tonight's speaker.

1 It was nice to have some p _ _ _ _ and quiet after the children had gone home.
2 The doctor said I should get some rest and r _ _ _ _ _ _ _ _ _.
3 There are car parks here and t _ _ _ _ in the city centre. Just look out for the signs.
4 I've been travelling back and f _ _ _ _ to London every day for the last three weeks.
5 It's been raining on and o _ _ all day.
6 This should be enough money for your meal, g _ _ _ or take a couple of euros.
7 He ran up and d _ _ _ the street looking for her.
8 She was ill in bed for two weeks but now she's out and a _ _ _ _ again.
9 Black and w _ _ _ _ photos can sometimes be more striking than coloured ones.
10 Ladies and g _ _ _ _ _ _ _ _, I'd like to propose a toast to the bride and groom.

Your score
/35

Abbreviations and acronyms

77.1 **What do these abbreviations stand for?**

10 marks

Example BBC ...British Broadcasting Corporation....

1 CIA ....
2 WHO ....
3 BTW ....
4 FYI ....
5 ATM ....
6 NATO ....
7 AFAIK ....
8 MI6 ....
9 IMHO ....
10 AFK ....

77.2 **What are the full forms of these shortened words?**

8 marks

Example kilo *kilogram*

1 sci-fi ....
2 gig ....
3 high-tech ....
4 uni ....
5 air con ....
6 sat nav ....
7 mobile ....
8 carbs ....

77.3 **Give abbreviations to replace the underlined words.**

9 marks

Example Here's an <u>I owe you</u> for the money you lent me. *IOU*

1 Please get in touch <u>as soon as possible</u>.
2 We prefer to avoid <u>genetically modified</u> foods.
3 The discovery of <u>deoxyribonucleic acid</u> has had a major impact on medical science.
4 Don't forget to take some kind of <u>identity card</u> with you to the exam tomorrow.
5 It's the second time this year that James has gone <u>absent without leave</u>.
6 Banks usually advise customers to memorise and not write down their <u>personal identity numbers</u>.
7 People in northern countries are more likely to suffer from <u>seasonal affective disorder</u>.
8 The police would like to interview anyone with any knowledge of the whereabouts of Sarah Lane, <u>also known as</u> Sarah Fisher.
9 You may find the information you need on our <u>Frequently Asked Questions</u> webpage.

77.4 **How are these abbreviations pronounced?**

8 marks

Example NATO – *as a word,* /ˈneɪtəʊ/

1 laser
2 BRB
3 ID
4 radar
5 AWOL
6 ASAP
7 CUL8R
8 LOL

Your score

/35

78.1 Match an expression on the left with a suitable sentence on the right.

10 marks

Example The house has seen better days. [g] a It's none of your business.

1 Stop making a meal out of it. ☐ b She annoys everyone.

2 Why don't you take the weight off your feet? ☐ c It's been such a depressing day.

3 He's always on the make. ☐ d He's just found his keys in the fridge.

4 She really pulled a fast one. ☐ e You've been standing up all day.

5 Don't poke your nose in. ☐ f He's just in it for his own profit.

6 I'm over the moon. ☐ g It used to be very smart.

7 I'm really down in the dumps. ☐ h We were tricked out of the money.

8 I'm in the red. ☐ i I'm absolutely delighted with the news.

9 She's a pain in the neck. ☐ j I thought I had more in my account.

10 He's as daft as a brush sometimes. ☐ k It was only a small mistake.

78.2 Complete the sentences with the words from the box.

10 marks

| barking | days | dumps | gold | heavy | move | ~~neck~~ | red | stick | weather | weight |

Example Jeremy's a pain in the ....*neck*.......... I don't know how she puts up with him.

1 I'm afraid she's got hold of the wrong end of the .... Let me explain.

2 He's .... up the wrong tree. It was last week it happened, not this week.

3 There's no need to make such .... weather of the assignment. It's not that hard.

4 Let's make a .... It's getting very late and you've got to get up early tomorrow.

5 Matt's car has certainly seen better .... but it serves its purpose.

6 Dad has been feeling a bit under the .... for the last few days.

7 Do come in and take the .... off your feet – you must be exhausted.

8 If you go into the .... , the bank starts charging a ridiculous amount of interest.

9 This miserable weather makes everyone feel a bit down in the ....

10 The children were as good as .... all day long.

78.3 Choose the correct words in these sentences.

10 marks

Example I wonder why Felipe is looking so down *on* /*in* the dumps.

1 I think he *barks / is barking* up the wrong tree, don't you?

2 This hotel *has seen / is seeing* better days.

3 It's time we *did / made* a move, I think.

4 Janek really *takes / is taking* the biscuit when it comes to being untidy.

5 Anya is feeling a bit *below / under* the weather today.

6 Don't make such a *dinner / meal* out of it – it's really not that important,

7 Selim's a clever boy but his twin's as daft as a *brush / broom*.

8 I wish he wouldn't try to poke his *nose / finger* into everything.

9 Claudio has always been *in / on* the make, always hoping to 'get rich quick'.

10 Don't imagine you can get away with *pulling / pushing* a fast one on me.

78.4 Answer the questions.

5 marks

Example If someone *pokes their nose into something*, are they being helpful or annoying?
  They're being annoying.

1 If children are *as good as gold*, are they well-behaved or naughty?

2 If someone *takes the weight off their feet*, do they stand up or sit down?

3 If someone is *over the moon*, do they feel happy or afraid?

4 If someone is *making heavy weather out of something*, are they finding it easy or difficult?

5 If someone is *barking up the wrong tree*, have they got hold of the wrong end of the stick or are they making a meal out of something?

Your score

/35

Words commonly mispronounced

79.1

10 marks

These words are in the IPA. Write their usual spellings.

Example /ˈɪntrəstɪŋ/ ...*interesting*..

1 /daʊt/ ....
2 /niː/ ....
3 /ˈresɪpiː/ ....
4 /ˈkʌbəd/ ....
5 /ɔːt/ ....
6 /ˈfɑːsən/ ....
7 /sɔːd/ ....
8 /kəˈtæstrəfɪ/ ....
9 /læm/ ....
10 /ˈsæmən/ ....

79.2

8 marks

Which of the three following words rhymes with the first word?

Example calm: tame, (farm), lamb

1 sorry: worry, lorry, hurry
2 love: stove, move, glove
3 friend: fiend, bend, fined
4 tomb: room, numb, foam
5 route: out, foot, root
6 chalk: park, sulk, walk
7 work: fork, jerk, talk
8 rein: pain, fine, seen

79.3

10 marks

Underline the stressed syllable in the words in bold.

Example Next week, we'll **prog**ress to the next stage.

1 What are your country's main **exports**?
2 They have **conflicting** ideas about their own roles.
3 The children have made a lot of **progress** with their maths.
4 The value of property usually **increases** every year.
5 Will they **permit** you to work there?
6 Although he's Russian, he has a UK permanent residence **permit**.
7 The highest July temperatures in London ever were **recorded** today.
8 'I'll never **desert** you,' the poet promised his beloved.
9 There is going to be an organised **protest** about the new by-pass.
10 What an **insult**! You have no right to speak to me like that.

79.4

7 marks

Underline the silent consonants in this text.

Joanna's a friend I met at my psychology class. She left the pretty comb I gave her for Christmas in the castle when we spent an hour there last week. She took it out of her bag because she wanted to get some knots out of her hair after we'd been walking outside in the wind. Then she must have dropped it. Luckily, an honest person picked it up and took it back to the information desk.

Your score

/35

Onomatopoeic words

80.1 Match the words on the left with suitable nouns on the right.

10 marks

Example mooing [k]   a lions
  1 buzzing ☐   b referee
  2 purring ☐   c dog
  3 roaring ☐   d birds
  4 crashing ☐   e fountain
  5 tweeting ☐   f salt
  6 growling ☐   g cymbals
  7 wheezing ☐   h bees
  8 spurting ☐   i breath
  9 sprinkling ☐   j cats
  10 whistling ☐   k cows

80.2 Choose the correct words in these sentences.

10 marks

Example The dog always *whistles / clashes /*(*growls*) when it sees the postman.

  1 Please can you help – you could *smash / mash / crash* the potatoes?
  2 Children love *spraying / spitting / splashing* through puddles.
  3 I woke to the sound of horses *clicking / spurting / clip-clopping* along the road.
  4 The wounded soldier *groaned / smashed / growled* in pain.
  5 Can you hear those church bells *clicking / clanging / clip-clopping*?
  6 She *sprayed / splashed / sprinkled* some herbs on the chicken.
  7 Sorry, I can't stop now. I've got to *whizz / dash / spit*.
  8 Can you *whistle / groan / grumble* this tune?
  9 I hate it when people *click / clang / sprinkle* their fingers to attract a waiter's attention.
  10 The children *bashed / grumbled / wheezed* about the amount of homework the teacher gave them.

80.3 Complete the sentences with the words from the box.

11 marks

grumpy   ~~tweet~~   gash   growl   moo   click
spit   whizz   wheeze   roar   meow   smash

Example In the spring, birds start to .....*tweet*..... very early in the morning.

  1 Champion tennis players .... the ball over the net with great power.
  2 I hate it when fierce dogs ....
  3 The attack left a .... in her arm.
  4 She's always a bit .... first thing in the morning.
  5 It's rude to .... in public places.
  6 Children sometimes .... back when cows make a noise.
  7 People with bronchitis tend to ....
  8 I heard several police cars .... by.
  9 She heard a .... at the end of the phone line as the caller hung up.
  10 Cats .... to tell you they're hungry.
  11 As well as lions, we say that aircraft or car engines ....

80.4 Match the combinations of letters with their usual associations.

4 marks

Example gr- [c]   a movement of water
  1 cl- ☐   b fast, violent movement
  2 sp- ☐   c something unpleasant or miserable
  3 wh- ☐   d a sharp metallic sound
  4 -ash ☐   e movement of air

Your score

/35

Homophones and homographs

81.1
10 marks

Read the text and find five more examples of homophones and five more examples of homographs. Explain why they are homophones or homographs.

Example 'Sow' is a homograph of the verb 'to sow' (seeds). 'Weight' is a homophone of 'wait'.

Look at that fat sow! What a weight she must be! Heavier than lead! I've never seen anything like it though I've read about pigs that size. And there are two piglets underneath her. What a row they are making. If she rolls over on top of them, they won't live. They certainly need a big pen to house an animal like her.

81.2
10 marks

Write two words to match each pronunciation written in the IPA.

Example /feɪz/ ....*faze, phase*.........

  1 /ˈweðə/ ....
  2 /aʊə/ ....
  3 /fluː/ ....
  4 /breɪk/ ....
  5 /feə/ ....
  6 /grəʊn/ ....
  7 /eə/ ....
  8 /miːt/ ....
  9 /sʌm/ ....
10 /meɪl/ ....

81.3
5 marks

The book titles below contain a pun (a joke based on words). Explain why the titles are funny.

Example **What a Pane!** *Memoirs of a Glassmaker*
      'What a pain' meaning 'What a nuisance' is an everyday expression. A 'pane' is a large piece of glass.

1 **Tee Time**, *Autobiography of a Golf Instructor*
2 **Love at First Site**, *Romance on an Archaeological Dig*
3 **This Place has Soul**, *Reminiscences of a Fishmonger*
4 **Sail of the Century**, *The Account of a Memorable Voyage*
5 **And Sew On**, *The Life of a Theatre Wardrobe Mistress*

81.4
10 marks

Find a word in the box that rhymes with the underlined word(s) in each sentence. (You do not need to use all the words in the box.)

choose	juice	found	bed	grinned	I've	~~feed~~	
mouse	spooned	so	now	give	cows	nose	mind

Example Ahmed can be relied on to take the <u>lead</u>. *feed*

1 The <u>wind</u> blew the tree down. ....
2 Have you <u>wound</u> the grandfather clock today? ....
3 I heard the band playing <u>live</u>. ....
4 The new galleries <u>house</u> the more modern painters in the collection. ....
5 I love your <u>bow</u> tie. ....
6 The children stood in two <u>rows</u>. ....
7 After its operation the cat just lay there licking its <u>wound</u>. ....
8 Do you <u>use</u> *English Grammar in Use*? ....
9 At the end of the concert the orchestra took a <u>bow</u>. ....

Your score
/35

Uncountable nouns

82.1
10 marks

Are these nouns normally countable or uncountable? Tick the correct option.

	countable	uncountable
Example passport	✓	☐
1 currency	☐	☐
2 luggage	☐	☐
3 reservation	☐	☐
4 accommodation	☐	☐
5 flight	☐	☐
6 information	☐	☐
7 travel	☐	☐
8 visa	☐	☐
9 journey	☐	☐
10 transport	☐	☐

82.2
10 marks

Correct the mistakes in these sentences.

Example I have ~~an~~ interesting news for you. some

1 We're going to the shops tomorrow. I want to look at some new furnitures. Maria wants to choose some skiing equipments and Mei needs some papers for her printer. We'll probably spend lots of moneys.
2 After doing courses at school, Sanjiv found that he was making progresses and increasing his knowledges of geography. He looked forward to continuing his studies at university and perhaps, one day, doing some researches into the geography of his local area.
3 I really need some advices from you, as someone with a lot of experiences, before I take up the violin. Do you have any tips about buying an instrument? Are there any works by famous composers that are easy for a beginner? What kinds of musics would you recommend?

82.3
5 marks

Which of these food words are not normally used in the plural?

Example sugar

biscuit   bread   butter   cake   flour   pie   pizza   soup   spaghetti   steak   ~~sugar~~   sweet

82.4
10 marks

Choose the correct words in these sentences.

Example Picnic cups and plates are often made of (plastic)/ *glasses* / *cloth*.

1 Jack did some very interesting *knowledge* / *research* / *experience* for his doctoral thesis.
2 I have bought some great new word-processing *work* / *equipment* / *software* for my computer.
3 Although Ivan is very rich, he does not like to show off his *wealth* / *progress* / *poverty*.
4 The car seats are made of *stone* / *leather* / *glasses*, which is much more comfortable than *a* / *the* / – plastic .
5 I hope the *news* / *weather* / *transport* will be good tomorrow because I'm planning to go for a long walk.
6 It took Andy some time to find suitable *homework* / *accommodation* / *travel* in London.
7 When you go abroad, it's sensible to get some of the country's *currency* / *luggage* / *wealth* before you arrive there.
8 Would you like *these* / *some* / *many* spaghetti or rice with your chicken?
9 The bride's wedding dress was made from *a* / *many* / *some* cloth she had bought in India.

Your score
/35

83.1
10 marks

Circle ten more nouns that are normally only used in the plural.

(tights) binoculars trousers slippers sunglasses gloves traffic lights tongs
tweezers corkscrews emails pyjamas shears rulers swimming trunks overalls

83.2
10 marks

Label the pictures.

Example .....jeans......   3 ....   6 ....   9 ....

1 ....   4 ....   7 ....   10 ....

2 ....   5 ....   8 ....

83.3
10 marks

Write full versions of these sentences, making the verbs and pronouns singular or plural as appropriate.

Example Physics (*be*) a very difficult subject.
          Physics is a very difficult subject.

1 Darts (*be*) a good game if you are bored and just want to have some fun.
2 Economics (*be*) my best subject when I was at college.
3 The news (*be*) very bad, I'm afraid. Do you want to hear (*it / them*)?
4 The spaghetti (*be*) ready. I hope you're hungry because there (*be*) a lot of (*it / them*).
5 Looks (*be*) not the most important thing. What matters is a person's character.
6 Maths (*be*) compulsory at school and I hated (*it / them*).
7 The proceeds of the sale (*is going / are going*) to charity.
8 The new Australian TV series (*be*) very interesting, I think.
9 James's new lodgings (*be*) quite expensive but (*it / they*) (*be*) very convenient.
10 The company's new premises (*be*) more convenient than their old (*one / ones*).

83.4
5 marks

Complete the sentences with plural words that mean the same as the phrases in brackets.

Example The company's ....headquarters.... are in Switzerland. (main offices)

1 The .... in the new concert hall are very good. (quality of the sound)
2 We complained about the planning proposals to the .... but it didn't do any good. (people in power)
3 The .... of each chapter are outlined at the beginning of the book. (what's in it)
4 A dangerous criminal has escaped. The police have no idea of his .... (where he is)
5 Some of the .... on the lorry were damaged in the accident. (things to be bought and sold)

Your score

/35

Countable and uncountable nouns with different meanings

84.1
10 marks
Complete the sentences with the correct forms of the nouns in brackets: either countable (with *a /an* or in the plural) or uncountable (no *a /an* or plural form).

Example Would you like me to sprinkle ....pepper........ on your pizza? (pepper)

1 There was .... on the floor and I got a little piece of it in my foot. (glass)
2 I've bought some lovely .... to make a skirt for the party. (cloth)
3 Would you like .... ? My sister bought me a big box for my birthday? (chocolate)
4 Would you like .... or .... for dinner tonight? (fish, chicken)
5 Could I borrow .... ? My shirt is creased after being in a suitcase for so long. (iron)
6 There's .... at the back of the house. We could go for a walk there after dinner if you like. (wood)
7 As I arrived I saw .... walking around the garden. And that was in the middle of the city! (chicken)
8 Did you buy .... for the printer? I need to print something off. (paper)
9 We need some .... for water. Could you fetch some? (glass)

84.2
10 marks
Choose the correct words in these sentences.

Example I love Suzie's long black (hair) / *hairs*.

1 He bought me a great present – Shakespeare's complete *work / works* on CD ROM.
2 Look at all the dog's *hair / hairs* on your black skirt.
3 I love meeting *people / peoples* from different countries and different professions.
4 There tend to be more female students in university *art / arts* departments than in science departments.
5 We had some great *time / times* when we were travelling together. We had some particularly interesting *experience / experiences* in South America.
6 *Time / Times* passed very quickly when we were on holiday.
7 My uncle did some research into the languages of the different *people / peoples* of Siberia.
8 Have you been to that new modern *art / arts* museum yet?
9 All my brothers do very different *work / works*.

84.3
10 marks
What's the difference between ...

Example ... *glass* and *a glass*? 'Glass' is a material used for windows, for example; 'a glass' is an object we drink from.

1 ... *pepper* and *a pepper*?
2 ... *iron* and *an iron*?
3 ... *plant* and *a plant*?
4 ... *coffee* and *a coffee*?
5 ... *damage* and *damages*?

84.4
5 marks
What does someone want if they ask you for ...

Example ... a paper? *a newspaper*

1 ... a cloth?
2 ... a rubber?
3 ... some chocolate?
4 ... some chocolates?
5 ... some paper?

Your score

/35

Making uncountable nouns countable

85.1 Complete the sentences with the correct forms of the words from the box.

10 marks

article   breath   carton   gust   ~~fit~~   loaf   lump   means   puff   spot   stroke

Example James hit the desk in a ....*fit*........ of temper.

1 Put another .... or two of coal on the fire, please.
2 I'd like two .... of bread please and a .... of milk.
3 A sudden .... of wind blew my papers all over the garden.
4 Jo spends all day in the library but I don't believe she does a .... of work there.
5 It's very stuffy here. I'm dying for a .... of fresh air.
6 Customers are permitted to take up to six .... of clothing into the changing room.
7 When I was walking home, I felt the first few .... of rain and now it's pouring.
8 He took the cigarette out of his mouth and blew out a .... of smoke.
9 The donkey is the main .... of transport on the island.

85.2 Rewrite the text making all the uncountable nouns countable.

8 marks

Example You can travel around England using different transport.
          You can travel around England using different means of transport.

Before you visit England, let me give you some advice and some information. Don't take too much luggage with you but take some warm clothing. You never know whether you are going to get good weather or not. One day, you will have thunder, lightning and rain and the next it will be sunny.

85.3 Complete the sentences using *state of* and one of the abstract nouns from the box.

7 marks

~~agitation~~   health   tension   disrepair   emergency   flux   uncertainty   poverty

Example Jiang is in a ....*state of agitation*........ waiting for his exam results.

1 After the floods a .... was declared in the city.
2 The old school building needs renovation as it is in a ....
3 Emma is still in a .... as to whether she has got the job or not.
4 The recession means that more people are living in a .... than before.
5 Grandma has been in a poor .... for some time now.
6 Our plans are in a .... at the moment as Harry has decided to join us on our travels.
7 The city is in a .... after last night's street fighting.

85.4 Complete the sentences with the correct words. (The first letters are given.)

10 marks

Example A g u s t of wind blew my umbrella inside out.

1 The boy took a b _ _ _ _ of grass, stretched it between his thumbs and blew on it, making a loud screeching noise.
2 I'd like four s _ _ _ _ _ of the chocolate cake in the window, please.
3 After the fire at the factory, a c _ _ _ _ of smoke hung over the town for several days.
4 Could you get me a couple of b _ _ _ of that apple-scented soap when you're at the chemist's and a t _ _ _ of toothpaste too, please?
5 We saw a f _ _ _ _ of lightning and then, seconds later, heard a loud c _ _ _ of thunder.
6 It was a s _ _ _ _ _ of luck bumping into you in town today!
7 We've had a wonderful s _ _ _ _ of sunny weather this week.
8 There were several interesting i _ _ _ _ on the news this morning.

Your score

/35

86.1 Complete the sentences with the words from the box in the correct form (singular or plural).
10 marks

gang crowd pack ~~bunch~~ herd team cast shoal flock group swarm

Example Takumi bought Jameela a lovely ......*bunch*...... of flowers for her birthday.

1 There was a .... of sheep in one field and a .... of cows in the next.
2 The boat had a glass bottom and we could see .... of colourful fish swimming below us.
3 She was attacked by a .... of bees and got badly stung.
4 .... of hungry wolves wandered the streets looking for food.
5 A .... of thieves has stolen a number of paintings worth over a million euros.
   A .... of detectives is now on the scene looking for evidence.
6 There was a large .... of at least 500 people waving banners and protesting. A small
   .... of police officers was trying to control them.
7 You can see the names of the .... on page 3 of the play's programme.

86.2 Label the pictures using the words from the box.
6 marks

| set |
| row |
| range |
| stack |
| clump |
| ~~pair~~ |
| pile |

Example ......*a pair of birds*...... 2 .... 4 ....

1 ....   3 ....   5 ....
   ....

86.3 Rewrite the sentences replacing the underlined words with collective nouns.
6 marks

Example A <u>large number of dogs</u> were running around the field. *A pack of dogs ...*

1 The <u>people who work in this company</u> are mostly young people.
2 The <u>people who flew the plane</u> remained calm during the emergency landing.
3 The <u>ordinary people</u> have a right to know how government spends their taxes.
4 The <u>people who played together in the match</u> were congratulated by the captain.
5 The <u>people who acted in the film</u> were just ordinary people, not famous actors.
6 The <u>people who usually act in this theatre</u> are on strike and so there will be no performances.

86.4 What do you call ...
13 marks

Example ... a lot of goats in one field? ...*a herd of goats*......

1 ... lots of dirty clothes on the floor?
2 ... six identical glasses?
3 ... a large group of birds?
4 ... two shoes?
5 ... two or three apples?
6 ... 52 playing cards?
7 ... a large group of mackerel?

8 ... six or seven islands close together?
9 ... four or five bananas joined together?
10 ... a lot of dishes in the sink?
11 ... a number of experts working together?
12 ... a lot of logs beside a house?
13 ... pots and pans of different sizes but the same design?

Your score
/35

Containers and contents

87.1 Label the pictures.

Example ....*a tube*....   3 ....   6 ....   9 ....

1 ....   4 ....   7 ....   10 ....

2 ....   5 ....   8 ....

87.2 Explain the difference between the two phrases.

Example a barrel of oil and a can of oil

> *A barrel of oil is a large wood or plastic container holding many litres of oil;*
> *a can of oil is a metal container holding typically half a litre or one litre.*

1 *a bottle of milk* and *a crate of milk*
2 *a cup of tea* and *a packet of tea*
3 *a box of sweets* and *a jar of sweets*
4 *a shopping bag* and *a shopping basket*
5 *a carton of juice* and *a jug of juice*
6 *a pot of ointment* and *a tube of ointment*
7 *a bowl of ice cream* and *a tub of ice cream*
8 *a case of wine* and *a glass of wine*
9 *a packet of cards* and *a pack of cards*

87.3 Put the words from the box in the correct column.

chocolates   honey   instant coffee   tools   olives   matches   tea bags   ~~paper clips~~

a box of	a jar of
paper clips	

88.1 Complete the phrases with *do* or *make*.

10 marks

Example ......make...... a mistake

1	.... your homework	6	.... the housework
2	.... fun of something or someone	7	.... a suggestion
3	.... the cooking	8	.... a profit
4	.... an exercise	9	.... business
5	.... a good impression	10	.... a success of something

88.2 Complete the sentences with the correct prepositions or particles.

9 marks

Example These sentences have been made ....up......... to show how some phrasal verbs based on *do* and *make* are used.

1 Freddie made .... as soon as he saw Vicky coming round the corner.
2 We're doing .... our kitchen at the moment and I need to get more paint.
3 Being able to change our car will make .... not having a holiday.
4 We made .... the hills, hoping to find somewhere for our picnic there.
5 I couldn't do .... my mobile – I use it all the time.
6 Nick sent me a note yesterday but I can't make .... what he's written.
7 What do you make .... the new boss? I can't decide if I like her or not.
8 I think we were invited to the concert only to make .... the numbers in the audience.

88.3 Correct the mistakes in these sentences.

6 marks

Example The boy ~~did~~ a face when the teacher said the class was going to have a test. *made*

1 Have you done all your homeworks yet?
2 Try not to do too many careless mistakes in your arithmetic test.
3 I've got a lot of work to make this evening.
4 It's not easy to make a going of a new business these days.
5 Can I help you make the washing-up?
6 Mateusz has made the arrangement for our trip to Japan.

88.4 Complete the sentences with words from the box and expressions with *do* or *make*.

10 marks

allowances	the best	cup of tea	decision	fuss
loss	cooking	~~mistakes~~	your best	gardening	noise

Example I was very pleased because I ..did.'t..make..any..mistakes. in the test.

1 The business .... last year but we hope it'll do better this year.
2 Dad's trying to sleep. Please don't ....
3 Emily's very good at .... of a bad situation.
4 The most important thing is to .... in the exam; it doesn't matter whether you get top marks or not.
5 Older children have to learn to .... for the fact that their younger brothers and sisters cannot do as much as they can.
6 I love trying out different recipes so I usually .... at home.
7 I don't know which university to choose but I'll have to .... soon.
8 You must .... this weekend – weed the flower beds, mow the lawn, that sort of thing.
9 I'll .... Then we can decide what to do while we're drinking it.
10 Alex was a bit jealous because everyone was .... of his new baby sister.

Your score

/35

89.1 Underline the phrasal verb in each sentence and suggest a synonym.

10 marks

Example She <u>brought</u> up six children all on her own. *raised*

1 The government has promised to bring down petrol prices soon.
2 Rachel takes after her mother in looks but her father in temperament.
3 The scandal may well bring down the government.
4 I wonder if they will ever bring back corporal punishment.
5 Don't be taken in by his easy charm. He's got a cruel streak.
6 The difficulties suffered during the war eventually brought about a revolution.
7 They're bringing out a new version of their mobile phone next month.
8 She's trying to bring her husband round to the idea of moving to Rome.
9 Adam wishes he could take back his angry words.
10 We took to each other at once and speak on the phone almost daily now.

89.2 Rewrite these sentences using expressions with *take* or *bring* (in the correct form) and the words in brackets.

10 marks

Example The play is set in a castle in Denmark. (place)
    The play takes place in a castle in Denmark.

1 It's right that this affair should be made public. (open)
2 I hope they won't exploit you. (advantage)
3 The research revealed some interesting facts. (light)
4 His rudeness astounded me. (breath)
5 You must think about applicants' experience as well as their qualifications. (consideration)
6 I always assumed that you'd become a lawyer like your parents. (granted)
7 The new laws will soon become law. (force)
8 Going out on your own at this time of night is risky. (risk)
9 Rick immediately started organising the situation. (control)
10 It's hard not to laugh at Dan's ideas. (seriously)

89.3 Complete the text with the correct prepositions / particles.

15 marks

Sophie was brought ....up......... in England. When she was 17, she went to visit an aunt in New York. She was nervous when her flight to New York took (1)...................... six hours late and the cold New York winter brought (2)...................... a nasty cold. But she soon began to feel at home and started taking the city (3)...................... granted. Living in New York really brought (4)...................... the best (5)...................... Sophie. She particularly enjoyed going to the Broadway theatre. She had always enjoyed taking other people (6)...................... and now she decided to take (7)...................... drama when she returned to England and went to college. She did all she could to take (8)...................... everything she was taught at college and she also took great pride (9)...................... her performances in student plays and was so successful that a professional theatre company was keen to take her (10)...................... . The theatre is a difficult career and Sophie's father was against her becoming an actor. Things were brought (11)...................... a head by the company's offer of work. Eventually Sophie managed to bring her father (12)...................... , especially as the theatre company said they were confident she had more chance than most of bringing it (13)...................... . She had minor parts for the first six months or so but then took (14)...................... a lead role. Indeed Sophie's career has really taken (15)...................... and she's now becoming quite famous all over the world.

Your score
/35

90.1 Match the beginning of each sentence with its ending.

10 marks

Example I hope Harvey will get through ☐ *i*   **a** to know her properly.

1 Sarah certainly got out of bed ☐   **b** to speak to him.

2 Our new flat is tiny so we must get ☐   **c** on the wrong side today.

3 Fortunately, the party got ☐   **d** through all my savings.

4 You'll love Mia once you get ☐   **e** into a good university last year.

5 Sonya is determined to get her ☐   **f** rid of our big sofa.

6 Tom was at the talk but I didn't get ☐   **g** to sorting out all your papers.

7 I won't be able to get out ☐   **h** own back on Joe for tricking her.

8 It didn't take long to get ☐   **i** all his exams.

9 Ned studied hard and got ☐   **j** off to a good start.

10 It's hard to get round ☐   **k** of Saturday's meeting.

90.2 Explain what *get* means in each of these sentences.

10 marks

Example What mark did you get in your exam? *receive*

1 I got these shoes in the sales.

2 How are you getting to Guy's party?

3 Gran seems to have got a lot older over this last year.

4 Why does he behave like that? I just don't get it.

5 Did you get the right answer to question 4?

6 His tuneless whistling really gets me.

7 I'll get dinner tonight but could you get something to drink?

8 I only got to know Julie last month but we've already got very close.

90.3 Correct the mistakes in these sentences.

5 marks

Example I'd like to ~~get knowing~~ my neighbours better. *get to know*

1 I wish I could get out my dental appointment tomorrow! I hate having my teeth filled.

2 Unfortunately, Viktor and I got to a bad start off.

3 I'm trying to think of a way to get the own back on Dave for lying to me.

4 You obviously got out of bed on the left side today!

5 We're getting very well on with the project now.

90.4 Choose the correct words in these sentences.

10 marks

Example The detective managed to get *with* /*at* the information he needed.

1 I hate this grey weather; it really gets me *down* / *off*.

2 We enjoyed Kim's *get-together* / *get-go* last night.

3 It won't take him very long to get *back* / *over* the operation.

4 I wonder what the children are getting *on* / *up* to now.

5 It'll be hard to catch up if you get *back* / *behind* with your work.

6 My sister's children are all getting *on* / *down* very well at college.

7 Not all lecturers are good at getting their points *across* / *off*.

8 It won't take long for Joe's promotion to get *across* / *round* the office.

9 I don't know how I'm going to get *over* / *on* without Kristin to help me.

10 All the children got *down* / *up* to work at once.

Your score

/35

Expressions with *set* and *put*

91.1
10 marks

Explain the meanings of the underlined expressions in the text.

Example has set her heart on becoming *very much wants to become*

My friend Lauren <u>has set her heart on becoming</u> a jazz singer but her father [1] <u>has put his foot down</u>. He is [2] <u>putting pressure on</u> her to do a catering course first. Lauren's twin brother Josh has [3] <u>set his sights on becoming</u> a politician. He and his friends spend hours drinking coffee and [4] <u>putting the world to rights</u>. The twins' father, however, would like to [5] <u>put a stop to</u> Josh's plans too. He wants Josh to [6] <u>set aside</u> his dreams and to [7] <u>put his mind to</u> developing a more secure career. Ideally, he would like the twins to [8] <u>set up</u> a hotel business together. He can't seem to [9] <u>put his ideas across</u>, however, and his attempts to persuade them to his point of view have only [10] <u>put their backs up</u> and made them more determined to stick to their original plans.

91.2
9 marks

Complete the expressions with *set* or *put*.

Example .... *set* .... your sights on

1 .... a good example
2 .... two and two together
3 .... a new record
4 .... on an accent
5 .... free

6 .... foot in
7 a .... -up job
8 .... a target
9 .... fire to

91.3
9 marks

Complete the sentences with the correct prepositions / particles.

Example What time do we need to set .... *off* .... for the airport?

1 You should put that proposal .... to the management committee.
2 If you put .... applying to college much longer, it'll be too late.
3 Most people try to set .... some money for their retirement if they can.
4 Children, help me put all your toys .... , please. We need to tidy this room.
5 Do you think you could put me .... when I come to London next weekend? It'd just be for one night.
6 A spider crawled across the sensor and set .... the burglar alarm.
7 Whenever Joe puts .... a remark, it's always to the point.
8 I hope my staying here isn't putting you .... too much?
9 The café has decided to put .... its prices for hot drinks.

91.4
7 marks

Complete the sentences with the correct forms of the phrasal verbs from the box.

put up   set out   put on   ~~set up~~   put down   put off   put together   put up with

Example Would you like to .... *set up* .... your own business one day?

1 I can't .... that loud music from next door any longer. I'm going round to have a word with them.
2 I hope that the difficult journey you had today won't .... you .... coming here again soon.
3 Could you help me .... this bookcase ....? The instructions aren't at all clear.
4 Max didn't .... to hurt Carola but he certainly succeeded in doing so.
5 I hate the way Steve likes to .... others .... with his sarcastic comments.
6 You could .... a notice advertising your car in the newsagent's.
7 The children are going to .... a concert at the end of term.

Your score
/35

92.1 Complete the sentences with the correct forms of *come* or *go*.

10 marks

Example Let's ......*go*...... through the plans once more.

1 This tie doesn't really .... with that shirt.
2 It is always hard to .... to terms with a death in the family.
3 It .... without saying that we'll give her a birthday present.
4 A lot of businesses .... bankrupt last year.
5 I wonder how Phil .... by that black eye?
6 The story .... that King Henry VIII once slept in that bed.
7 Gemma's exam results .... out yesterday morning.
8 I wasn't sure which skirt to choose but in the end I .... for the red one.
9 A number of interesting points .... up at yesterday's meeting.
10 I'm nearly ready. You .... on and I'll catch you up in a few minutes.

92.2 Match the underlined expressions in the text with the definitions in the box.

10 marks

Example goes without saying *is obvious*

are enthusiastic about become fashionable busy continuing do anything found getting a contract ~~is obvious~~ make a success separate within its limitations

It <u>goes without saying</u> that I hope that Emma and Chris will ⁽¹⁾ <u>make a go</u> of their marriage. However, I am sure that no wife or family will ever ⁽²⁾ <u>come between</u> Chris and his music. Ever since he first ⁽³⁾ <u>came across</u> an old guitar in a secondhand shop, Chris has been passionate about playing. He'll ⁽⁴⁾ <u>go to great lengths</u> to improve, often ⁽⁵⁾ <u>going on</u> practising the same pieces until late at night, even when he's been ⁽⁶⁾ <u>on the go</u> at work all day long. He has great hopes of ⁽⁷⁾ <u>coming to an agreement</u> with a recording company but, although his playing is very good ⁽⁸⁾ <u>as far as it goes</u>, not many people really ⁽⁹⁾ <u>go for</u> his style of music at the moment. Who knows if it will ever ⁽¹⁰⁾ <u>come into fashion</u> again?

92.3 Put the words from the box in the correct columns: those that collocate with *come to* and those that collocate with *come into*.

10 marks

contact with a decision a fortune a standstill view an end existence ~~fashion~~ operation sight a conclusion

come to	come into
	fashion

92.4 Correct the mistakes in these sentences.

5 marks

Example He really ~~went her for~~ when she said he was wrong. *went for her*

1 Milly has come with up some very good ideas for the party.
2 I wouldn't want to go such a terrible experience through again.
3 The boss is always going at me on about my untidy desk.
4 Would you like to come to my house round this evening?
5 I hope the proposal will go without any problems through.

Your score

/35

Expressions with other common verbs

93.1 Complete the sentences with the correct forms of the verbs from the box. (Nearly all
the verbs are used twice.)

Example You shouldn't ......*turn*...... down such a generous offer of help.

| break |
| let |
| look |
| run |
| see |
| turn |

1 I'm .... into the possibility of going to Australia next year.
2 I'm going to .... out of printer paper soon.
3 Gary soon .... through Adèle's plans to trick him.
4 When the police .... into the case, they decided to charge Jones with
   the theft.
5 Trains don't .... from Wiggleton to Camthorpe on a Sunday.
6 We'll need to .... about booking our summer holiday soon.
7 It was a lovely surprise when my nephews .... up last weekend.
8 I will finish the job properly. I promise I won't .... you down.
9 Kay was in the middle of a sentence when she suddenly .... off as Leila appeared.
10 I'm sure Jurg would never .... his promise to look after you.

93.2 Complete the sentences with the expressions from the box.

| broke the record   broke her heart   ~~let it slip~~   looks down on   on the bright side |
| over a new leaf   let off   in the long run   seeing things   take turns at   break the news |

Example Hannah ....*let it slip*..... last night that she's been offered a new job.

1 Lidya has a very positive attitude. She always looks ....
2 My flatmates and I .... cooking the evening meal.
3 Isabel tends to be untidy but she is trying to turn ....
4 Charles is an intellectual snob. He .... people with little education.
5 This paper was the first to .... about the corruption scandal.
6 The accused was .... with a warning.
7 A South African athlete .... for the long jump.
8 That surely can't be Meriel. We must be ....
9 Setting up your own business won't be easy but it'll be worth it ....
10 When Nick left his girlfriend, it ....

93.3 Choose from the box. What are . . .

| a holiday   a job   firefighters   ~~someone's hand~~   ~~a rope~~   sugar   a party   news |
| professional sportsmen and women   an invitation   promises   petrol |

Example ... two things people might let go of? *someone's hand, a rope*

1 ... two things people run out of?
2 ... two things people look forward to?
3 ... two things that people turn down?
4 ... two types of people that are looked up to?
5 ... two things that people can break?

93.4 Answer the questions and explain your answers.

Example If you *turn over a new leaf*, are you doing some gardening?
     No, you're trying to change a bad habit.

1 Do pop singers like it if a lot of people *turn up* to hear them play?
2 If you say someone's *seeing things*, do you mean that they're long-sighted?
3 If you *run into someone*, do you hurt yourself?
4 Where do you usually *see someone off*?
5 If a painting *turns out to be* a fake, has it always been known that it was a fake?

Your score
/35

94.1 Put the words in the correct columns.

10 marks

> ~~goodbye~~ kids go amiss offspring children abode house go pear-shaped go wrong cheerio bye-bye

formal	neutral	informal
goodbye		

94.2 Match the formal words on the left with their neutral / informal equivalents on the right.

8 marks

Example attempt - try

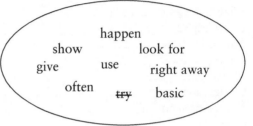

fundamental
~~attempt~~ occur utilise
immediately establish
provide
seek
frequently

happen
show look for
give use right away
often ~~try~~ basic

94.3 Correct the mistakes in these sentences. (2 mistakes in each sentence)

10 marks

Example Tickets must be ~~purchase~~ purchased before ~~board~~ boarding the bus.

1 The subway is closed until furthest notices.
2 Do not adress the driver unless the bus is stationery.
3 Do not alighten while the bus is in moving.
4 Articles deposed here must be paid for on advance.
5 We regret not longer to accept cheques.

94.4 Complete the sentences with the correct prepositions.

7 marks

Example Greene argues that young children, ...*in*......... particular, need to have a
regular routine.

1 South Africa provides the world .... gold and diamonds.
2 .... terms .... job opportunities, things are not as easy for graduates as they once were.
3 Paul used the map to work out where he was in relation .... the village.
4 I worked things out .... the basis of the figures I was given.
5 Fewer students are applying to study medicine .... account .... the increase in fees for medical school.

Your score

/35

Formal and informal words 2

95.1 Put these slang words in the correct circles.

10 marks

anorak ~~bread~~ cuppa dosh grub nerd nosh quack readies squaddie the bill

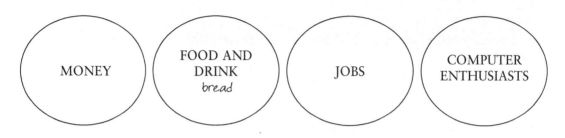

MONEY

FOOD AND DRINK
bread

JOBS

COMPUTER ENTHUSIASTS

95.2 Write the shorter, more informal versions of these words.

10 marks

Example to telephone *to phone*

1 laboratory ....
2 celebrity ....
3 mobile phone ....
4 refrigerator ....
5 magazine ....
6 television ....
7 advertisement ....
8 veterinary surgeon ....
9 newspaper ....
10 bicycle ....

95.3 Read the sentences and answer the questions using neutral words.

6 marks

Example *I've got a great new bike.* What has the speaker just bought? *a bicycle*

1 *His uncle is in the nick.*   Where is his uncle?
2 *Can you buy me some spuds?*   What does the speaker need?
3 *I'd take the tube if I were you.*   How does the speaker recommend travelling?
4 *I need another five quid.*   What does the speaker want?
5 *There are a lot of cops in the street.*   What can the speaker see?
6 *Shall we call a cab now?*   What does the speaker suggest?

95.4 Complete the sentences with the words from the box.

9 marks

ads anorak dosh nosh cuppa loo cops mobile vet ~~squaddie~~

Example Lena's met a nice young ......*squaddie*...... who's based at the local army barracks.

1 You have to take a cat to the .... every year for a vaccination.
2 Look in the local paper's classified .... section, if you want to rent a flat.
3 They serve great .... in that restaurant.
4 Sit down, put your feet up and I'll make a nice ....
5 He's nice but a bit of an .... , always talking about computers and stuff.
6 Could you call my .... from yours. I'm trying to find it.
7 Sorry I took so long – there was a queue for the ....
8 Lisa called the .... as soon as she realised the flat had been broken into.
9 I haven't got much .... on me. Can you lend me £20 till tomorrow?

Your score
/35

96.1 Complete the similes with the words from the box.

10 marks

~~blind~~ bold bone bull deaf drunk fish horse iron mad ox

Example as ....blind.......... as a bat

1 as .... as a lord
2 as .... as a hatter
3 as .... as a post
4 to eat like a ....
5 as hard as ....
6 as dry as a ....
7 as strong as an ....
8 to drink like a ....
9 as .... as brass
10 to behave like a .... in a china shop

96.2 Agree with the following statements. Use similes.

5 marks

Example Mo's very tanned after her holiday.
  Yes, she's as brown as a berry.

1 The children behaved very well yesterday.
2 Toby never has too much to drink, does he?
3 Didn't he blush when she looked at him!
4 Zack never says a word, does he?
5 I couldn't believe how little she weighs.

96.3 What do the similes in these sentences mean?

10 marks

Example The exam was as easy as falling off a log.
  The exam was very easy.

1 I slept like a log.
2 He was as sick as a dog all night.
3 The goalkeeper was as sick as a parrot after the match.
4 When she heard the news she went as white as a sheet.
5 The lady's hands were as white as snow.
6 Our plan worked like a dream.
7 My father has eyes like a hawk.
8 Steve is like a bear with a sore head today.
9 I'm sorry I forgot. I've got a head like a sieve.
10 She's only small but she eats like a horse.

96.4 Rewrite these sentences using similes with *as* or *like* and the word(s) in brackets.

10 marks

Example I was terribly sick after eating all those sausages last night. (dog)
  I was as sick as a dog after eating all those sausages last night.

1 She's very thin but very strong. (rake, ox)
2 He's in a very bad temper today. (bear)
3 He's terribly forgetful and is completely mad. (mind, hatter)
4 His grandmother notices everything that we do. (hawk)
5 She looked really cool even though it was 30° in the shade. (cucumber)
6 My plan worked very well and the work was done very quickly. (dream, flash)
7 Party political broadcasts on TV make my dad furious. (bull)

Your score

/35

97.1 Complete the proverbs with the correct words. (The first letters are given.)

10 marks

Example One s <u>w a l l o w</u> doesn't make a summer.

1 Never judge a b _ _ _ by its c _ _ _ _ .
2 You can lead a h _ _ _ _ to w _ _ _ _ but you can't make it d _ _ _ _ .
3 Too many c _ _ _ _ spoil the b _ _ _ _ .
4 People who live in g _ _ _ _ houses shouldn't t _ _ _ _ stones.
5 We'll cross that b _ _ _ _ _ when we come to it.

97.2 Correct the mistakes in these sentences. Then match each sentence with its explanation a–k.

20 marks

Example Don't count your ~~ducklings~~ chickens before they hatch. ☐ k

1 Don't put all your apples in one basket. ☐

2 When the cat's away, the dogs will play. ☐

3 Never look a gift horse in the eyes. ☐

4 There's no smoke without cigarettes. ☐

5 Many fingers make light work. ☐

6 Take care of the pennies and the dollars will take care of themselves. ☐

7 One swallow doesn't make a spring. ☐

8 Never judge a book by its writer. ☐

9 Too many cooks spoil the dinner. ☐

10 We'll cross that street when we come to it. ☐

a Don't anticipate future problems before they happen.

b Take care of small sums of money and they'll become large sums.

c People sometimes take advantage of the person in authority being absent.

d Don't judge people or things by their outward appearance.

e One positive sign doesn't mean that everything will be good.

f Extra problems can arise if too many people are involved.

g Don't refuse good fortune when it's there in front of you.

h Rumours are often based on an element of truth.

i Don't invest all your efforts or attention in just one thing.

j Things are easier when there are a lot of people to help.

k Don't assume in advance that your plans will all work out well.

97.3 Which of the proverbs from 97.1 and 97.2 might you use in these situations?

5 marks

Example A lot of people are helping to decorate a room for a party and things are beginning to look a bit of a mess. Too many cooks spoil the broth.

1 An extravagant person criticises you for buying an expensive car.
2 A rumour is going round about corruption in government.
3 A parent has taken their children to France but the children won't practise speaking French.
4 Your friend is worried that she might have her passport stolen when you're on holiday together.
5 The teacher leaves the classroom and the children immediately stop working.

Your score
/35

98.1 Where might you see these signs? What do they mean?

10 marks

✓FISHING
PERMIT HOLDERS ONLY

Example by a river / lake; Only people with special cards giving them permission are allowed to fish here.

1
REDUCE SPEED NOW

2 THIS PACKET CARRIES A GOVERNMENT HEALTH WARNING

3
P PAY AND DISPLAY

4
Trespassers will be prosecuted

5 **NO** ADMISSION TO UNACCOMPANIED MINORS

98.2 Match the words and phrases on the left with their everyday equivalents.

11 marks

Example trespassers e

1 alight ☐   a get off (a bicycle or horse)
2 purchases ☐   b take to court
3 personnel ☐   c get off (a bus or train)
4 prohibited ☐   d young people not yet legally adult
5 penalty ☐   e people who go somewhere illegally
6 refrain ☐   f moving
7 minors ☐   g things you are buying / have bought
8 in motion ☐   h punishment, fine
9 dismount ☐   i people
10 unauthorised ☐   j do not
11 prosecute ☐   k without official permission
              l forbidden

98.3 Put the words in the correct order to make typical notices. What does each one mean?

14 marks

Example HERE SPOKEN SPANISH

Spanish spoken here. Some of the staff here speak Spanish.

1 prohibited the feeding is animals strictly ....
2 here your place purchases ....
3 motor through no vehicles for road ....
4 from refrain in kindly phones using auditorium the mobile ....
5 whilst not bus alight do the it in from is motion ....
6 will shoplifters prosecuted be ....
7 to admission holders only ticket ....

99.1

10 marks

Match one word from each headline with one word from the box.

> affect   approval   attempt   clever activity   conflict
> encourage   fire   ~~investigation~~   marry   promise   request

Example TAX <u>PROBE</u> REVEALS FRAUD *investigation*

1 NEW INTEREST RATES BOOST SALES ....
2 FILM STAR TO WED VICAR ....
3 MORE STRIFE AT FACTORY ....
4 BY-PASS PLANS GET GO-AHEAD ....
5 STORMS HIT REGION ....
6 BLAZE AT LOCAL SCHOOL ....
7 MOTHER'S PLEA FOR HELP ....
8 HUSBAND'S FINAL VOW ....
9 PRISONERS' SECRET PLOY ....
10 NEW BID TO CONQUER EVEREST ....

99.2

12 marks

Explain the meanings of the underlined words in these headlines.

Example TV BOSS <u>QUITS</u> *leaves his job*

1 MINISTER <u>BACKS</u> PEACE <u>MOVES</u>
2 TV <u>POLL</u> PUBLISHED
3 TAKEOVER <u>TALKS</u> FAIL
4 COURTROOM <u>DRAMA</u> ENDS
5 <u>GEMS</u> COMPANY <u>HEAD</u> TO GO
6 SON <u>VOWS</u> TO <u>OUST</u> DAD
7 PRINCE <u>PLEDGES</u> SUPPORT FOR TAX <u>CUTS</u>
8 JOBS <u>THREAT</u> AT FACTORY

99.3

8 marks

Read the headlines and answer the questions.

Example NEW COMPANY BOSS ANNOUNCED What has just been announced?
> *The new head of a company*

1 FACTORY BLAST KILLS FIVE   What killed five people?
2 GEMS THEFT FROM STAR'S FLAT   What did the star lose?
3 AID PROMISED TO FAMINE VICTIMS   What has been promised?
4 GIRL IN TRAIN ORDEAL   Was the girl's experience easy or difficult?
5 ANONYMOUS LETTER RIDDLE   How do people feel about the anonymous letter?
6 CLASH AT THEATRE   What happened at the theatre?
7 KEY WORKERS GET PAY RISE   Which workers have had a pay rise?
8 CURB ON CITY PARKING   What is happening to parking in the city?

99.4

5 marks

Explain the pun (i.e. play on words) in each headline.

Example SKI POLL ANNOUNCED
> *A ski pole (pronounced the same as 'poll' = survey) is one of
> the two sticks that a skier uses to help him or her move.*

1 TREE BOSS AXED
2 MAFIA GOLF LINKS
3 SCHOOLS' CHOCOLATE BAR
4 ROAD RAGE DRIVE
5 TRAFFIC WARDENS CURBED

Your score

/35

100.1
10 marks

Complete the crossword by writing the US equivalents of the British words in clues 1–11.

Across

1 colour
4 rubbish
6 ~~flat~~
9 single (ticket)
10 bonnet (of a car)
11 wardrobe

Down

2 queue
3 holiday
5 toilets
7 garden
8 petrol

100.2
7 marks

Write the British and the US words for these things.

Example bonnet (Br) /
hood (US)

2 ....

4 ....

6 ....

1 ....

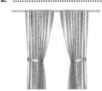

3 ....

5 ....

7 ....

100.3
10 marks

Explain what (a) a British person and (b) someone from the USA means when they say:

Example Jack has gone to buy some new pants.
    (a) an item of underwear (b) some trousers

1 Would you like to wash up?
2 We live on the first floor.
3 He's wearing a very old vest.
4 Did you use the subway today?
5 Can I have my bill, please?

100.4
8 marks

Write the US equivalents of these British English words.

Example film ....*movie*.........

1 biscuit ....
2 car park ....
3 pavement ....
4 sellotape ....

5 sweets ....
6 return (ticket) ....
7 zebra crossing ....
8 lift ....

Your score
/35

Answer key

Test 1

1.1 a sense of humour; a train set; at a loss for words; common sense; a remarkable coincidence; to coin a phrase; a subtle difference; a royal palace; to express an opinion; to take sides (10 marks)

1.2 1 e   2 f   3 a   4 d   5 c   (5 marks)

1.3 1 scissors   2 text   3 express   4 chemist   5 to alight   (5 marks)

1.4 1 rectangle   2 screwdriver   3 coin   4 sunshade   5 comb   (5 marks)

1.5 **things you can read:** blogs, magazines, tweets, encyclopedias, recipes, comics
things you can watch / listen to: [TV], audio books, songs, DVDs, podcasts (10 marks)

Test 2

2.1
1 verb   4 fixed phrase   7 collocation   9 noun
2 adjective   5 adjective   8 collocation   10 fixed phrase
3 verb   6 adjective   (10 marks)

2.2 **music:** [piano], cello, folk, a track, release an album
the Internet: blog, the web, identity theft, social network, upload a video (9 marks)

2.3
1 A   3 A   5 S   7 S
2 S   4 S   6 A   8 S   (8 marks)

2.4

noun	verb	adjective
product, [produce]	*produce*	*productive*
practice	*practise*	practical
politics, *politician*		*political*
information	*inform*	informative

(8 marks)

Test 3

3.1
1 among   3 national   5 pleasure   7 mother   9 educational
2 church   4 thirteen   6 password   8 fascinating 10 asleep   (10 marks)

3.2
1 transitive   4 stress   7 antonyms
2 collocation   5 intransitive   8 preposition
3 pronunciation   6 abbreviation   9 conjunction   (9 marks)

3.3
1 <u>ex</u>tract (noun)   3 ther<u>mo</u>meter   5 re<u>cord</u> (verb)
2 sup<u>ply</u>   4 <u>life</u>style   6 <u>record</u> (noun)   (6 marks)

3.4
1 The accused man denied ~~to steal~~ *stealing* the car.
2 The college will supply you ~~of~~ *with* a coursebook.
3 I suggest you ~~to~~ *revise* the first three units of this book before the test.
4 You shouldn't make such ~~hurtfull~~ *hurtful* remarks.
5 When are you going to get round to ~~tidy~~ *tidying* your bedroom? (10 marks – 1 for finding the mistake and 1 for correcting it)

Test 4

4.1
1 lacking in understanding or sympathy towards someone's suffering
2 stop producing
3 very busy, same meaning as *up to her eyes*

4 impossible to imagine
　　　5 against the government
　　　6 machine for making bread
　　　7 send again
　　　8 not inhabited; no one lives there
　　　9 before the wedding
　　10 period of sleep during the winter　　　　　　　　　　　　　　(10 marks)

4.2　1 type of laughing　　3 type of flower　　5 type of bird
　　　2 type of tool　　　　4 type of movement　　　　　　　　　(5 marks)

4.3　1 a case for keeping glasses (spectacles) in
　　　2 a basket for a cat to sleep in
　　　3 a spoon used for adding sugar to tea and stirring it; also used for
　　　　measuring ingredients when cooking
　　　4 a lane of the road that is meant to be used by buses rather than other traffic
　　　5 a stool to rest your feet on
　　　6 a dish to put butter in
　　　7 a machine for making ice cream
　　　8 a magazine about computers
　　　9 a thing for opening bottles
　　10 a light used for lighting a street　　　　　　　　　　　　　(10 marks)

4.4　1 ratty　　　　4 longevity　　7 lifespan　　9 nut-free
　　　2 unrecognisable　5 disconnect　8 unfinished　10 rewrite
　　　3 tended　　　　6 Superstitious　　　　　　　　　　　　(10 marks)

Test 5

5.1　1 the United Kingdom　　　6 – Canada
　　　2 – Australia　　　　　　7 the USA
　　　3 the Arctic　　　　　　8 – Poland
　　　4 the Philippines　　　　9 – Argentina
　　　5 – India　　　　　　　10 the United Arab Emirates　　　(10 marks)

5.2　1 Japanese　　4 Bangladeshi　7 Danish　　9 Icelandic
　　　2 Brazilian　　5 Korean　　　8 Turkish　10 Thai
　　　3 Irish　　　　6 Iraqi　　　　　　　　　　　　　　　(10 marks)

5.3　1 I think she married a French *man*.
　　　2 Do you speak any ~~Arab~~ *Arabic*?
　　　3 My sister was born in the ~~Central~~ *Middle* East, in Jordan to be precise.
　　　4 I plan to learn some ~~Greece~~ *Greek* before I go to live in Athens.
　　　5 Stand in this queue if you have ~~an~~ *a* European passport.
　　　6 I'd love to visit ~~the~~ Antarctica.
　　　7 I met some very nice ~~Finnish and Swedish~~ *Finns and Swedes* on holiday. OR I met some
　　　　very nice Finnish and Swedish *people* on holiday.
　　　8 Amsterdam is the capital of *the* Netherlands, even though The Hague is the seat of
　　　　government.
　　　9 Columbus sailed across the Atlantic to *the* Caribbean.
　　10 We had a wonderful holiday in the ~~Switzerland~~ *Swiss* mountains.　(10 marks)

5.4　1 monolingual　　　　　　　　4 dialects
　　　2 multilingual　　　　　　　　5 a Cypriot
　　　3 your mother tongue (or native / first language)　　　　　(5 marks)

Test 6

6.1 **cold weather:** freeze, frost, thaw
hot weather: boiling, heatwave, humid, stifling
wet weather: [torrential rain], downpour, flood, shower   (10 marks)

6.2
1 melts; thaws	5 severe / snowy	8 expects; late
2 breeze	6 drought	9 daytime
3 overcast; pour (down)	7 misty	10 heavy; flood
4 muggy		

(14 marks)

6.3 1 *damp*; the other words refer to heat
2 *drought*; the other words refer to wind
3 *frost*; the other words refer to rain   (6 marks – 1 for identifying the odd word out
and 1 for the explanation)

6.4 1 The rain was so heavy that several roads got ~~flood~~ *flooded*.
2 I haven't seen such ~~torrent~~ *torrential* rain for a very long time.
3 There was such a strong ~~windy~~ *wind* that my mum's hat blew off.
4 Do you have to go out in this ~~pourdown~~ *downpour*?
5 We had ~~a~~ very nice weather on our holiday.   (5 marks)

Test 7

7.1
1 bald; skin	4 beard; moustache; chubby
2 blonde; fair	5 straight; thin
3 curly	

(10 marks)

7.2
1 wavy	9 red
2 reddish-brown	10 less
3 plump	11 broad and solid
4 overweight	12 a tan
5 more	13 muscular
6 eating	14 19, 20, or 21
7 their body	15 nose, eyes, mouth, chin, cheek, forehead, lips, eyebrows
8 their face	

(15 marks)

7.3 1 N   2 P   3 P   4 N   5 P   6 N   7 P   8 N   9 P   10 P   (10 marks)

Test 8

8.1 impolite – discourteous; quarrelsome – argumentative; sensible – down-to-earth;
obstinate – stubborn; brusque – curt; cunning – sly; gifted – talented; trustworthy – reliable;
sociable – gregarious; tense – wound up   (10 marks)

8.2
1 Rob is envious.	5 Julia is jealous.	8 Emma's sensitive.
2 Suzie's easy-going.	6 Becky's eccentric.	9 Ali is extroverted.
3 Mickey's cruel.	7 Bob's nosy.	10 Maggie's brainless.
4 Clare's sincere.		

(10 marks)

8.3
1 A	3 DA	5 DA	7 A	9 DA
2 A	4 DA	6 A	8 DA	10 A

(10 marks)

8.4 1 unprincipled   2 weird   3 extravagant   4 determined   5 tight-fisted   (5 marks)

Test 9

9.1
1 sand	3 bones	5 pain	7 good	9 shoulders
2 ball	4 heights	6 place	8 pet	10 piece

(10 marks)

9.2
1 N	3 N	5 P	7 N	9 N
2 P	4 P	6 N	8 P	10 N (10 marks)

9.3
1 Izzy	3 Tom	5 Rita	7 Ben	9 Lee
2 Leila	4 Tessa	6 Zara	8 Mark	10 Victoria (10 marks)

9.4
1 annoy you	3 average	5 criticising
2 feel irritated by it	4 behaviour	(5 marks)

Test 10

10.1
1 T	3 F	5 T	7 F	9 F
2 T	4 T	6 F	8 T	10 F (10 marks)

10.2
1 I can't stand my new boss.
2 She's fallen out with her colleagues.
3 Jo and I are class-mates.
4 I think Rick's having an affair with his best friend's wife.
5 Bethany looks up to her older brother. (5 marks)

10.3
1 get; with	5 left	8 together
2 casual; acquaintance	6 partner	9 best; fell; see
3 adores	7 comments	10 steady
4 accept; interact		(15 marks)

10.4 1 do   2 make   3 to   4 on   5 parents-in-law   (5 marks)

Test 11

11.1
1 a corkscrew	6 (coat) hangers
2 a remote (control)	7 a powerpoint / socket
3 a phone charger	8 a dustpan and brush
4 an ironing board	9 a chopping board
5 (table) mats	10 a grater (10 marks)

11.2
1 loft; attic	5 utility room	9 hall(way)
2 master / main bedroom	6 cellar	10 drive
3 shed	7 basement	11 porch
4 patio; terrace	8 landing	(13 marks)

11.3 1 e   2 d   3 h   4 b   5 g   6 a   7 c   (7 marks)

11.4 1 patio   2 drive   3 loft conversion   4 shed   5 studio   (5 marks)

Test 12

12.1
1 crashed	4 twisted	7 flat	9 tripped
2 grazed	5 bang	8 stain	10 broke
3 stopped	6 mislaid		(10 marks)

12.2
1 j; keys	4 k; power	7 i; leaking	9 a; hot
2 f; dropped	5 c; flat	8 b; in	10 e; spilt
3 g; a hole	6 d; the coffee grounds		(20 marks)

12.3 1 d   2 f   3 b   4 a   5 e   (5 marks)

Test 13

13.1
1 damaged; injured	3 starved	5 civil; refugees
2 dead; wounded	4 erupted	6 accident; casualties (10 marks)

13.2 1 rabies   2 malaria   3 AIDS   4 cholera; typhoid   (5 marks)

13.3 STRONG WINDS: [hurricane], tornado, typhoon
LAND MOVEMENT: earthquake, landslide, volcano
WET / DRY: drought, flood
PEOPLE: casualty, survivor, victim   (10 marks)

13.4
1 shook	4 swept	7 starved
2 spread	5 damaged	8 suffered
3 broke	6 injured; erupted	9 wounded

(10 marks)

Test 14

14.1
1 False. *To pass an exam* means the same as *to do well in an exam. To do or take an exam* means the same as *to sit an exam.*
2 True
3 True
4 False. A comprehensive school is for all pupils.
5 False. A crèche is for babies and very small children.
6 True
7 False. A university is usually more academic than a college.
8 True
9 False. A workshop is a class that usually focuses on practical skills but these could be in relation to all sorts of subjects, e.g. dance, writing, art, drama, etc. (also sometimes even business skills).
10 True   (10 marks)

14.2 continuous assessment; teacher-training college; blended learning; graduation ceremony; school-leaving age; primary school; post-graduate degree   (7 marks)

14.3
1 skip; do	3 mark	5 degree	7 submit	9 grant
2 pass	4 thesis	6 admission	8 Compulsory	

(10 marks)

14.4
1 monitor	3 failed	5 progress	7 secondary
2 module	4 dissertation	6 graduate	8 grammar

(8 marks)

Test 15

15.1
1 What does your sister do ~~to~~ *for* a living?
2 The union is encouraging its members to go ~~in~~ *on* strike.
3 Orla is ~~in~~ *on* flexi-time so she usually gets to work at 7 and leaves at 3.
4 My sister has got a new job as a ~~publicity~~ *public* relations officer.
5 I go to ~~job~~ *work* by bike most days.
6 When the company was taken over several staff were laid ~~out~~ *off*.
7 Maria expects to be promoted to a new ~~work~~ *job* soon.
8 The interests of the staff are defended by two ~~unions~~ *union* representatives.
9 Will you take the job if you are ~~offering~~ *offered* it?
10 A child-minder looks ~~for~~ *after* other people's children in her own home.   (10 marks)

15.2 **professions:** [banker], diplomat, economist, judge, physiotherapist, scientist
trades: carpenter, electrician, firefighter, plumber, receptionist   (10 marks)

15.3
1 g	3 h	5 i	7 b	9 e
2 k	4 a	6 c	8 j	10 f

(10 marks)

15.4
1 a workaholic	3 a civil servant	5 a director
2 maternity leave	4 an unskilled worker	

(5 marks)

Test 16

16.1 to launch a new range; worth the risk; customer care; to make a profit; market research; to do business; a business plan; stiff competition; order books; to build contacts   (10 marks)

16.2
1 manufacture	4 expand	7 corporation	9 feedback
2 priority	5 potential	8 roll out	10 recession
3 put forward	6 custom-built		(10 marks)

16.3
1 forward	4 Executive	7 custom-	9 books
2 access	5 launch	8 contacts	10 the risk
3 sell	6 out		(10 marks)

16.4   1 a profit   2 businesses   3 profits   4 business   5 profits   (5 marks)

Test 17

17.1
1 table tennis	4 motor racing	7 snow-boarding	9 windsurfing
2 ten-pin bowling	5 archery	8 hang-gliding	10 scuba-diving
3 fencing	6 canoeing		(10 marks)

17.2
1 a tennis player	4 an archer	7 a jockey	9 a squash player
2 a canoeist	5 a sprinter	8 a footballer	10 a swimmer
3 a gymnast	6 a mountaineer		(10 marks)

17.3
1 referee	4 sports	7 knocked; round
2 set	5 trophy	8 spectator
3 make	6 qualified	9 final (10 marks)

17.4   1 a bat   2 a stick   3 a bat   4 oars   5 a cue   (5 marks)

Test 18

18.1   literature: 1 poetry, 4 novels, 8 biographies
fine art: 2 ceramics, 5 sculpture, 7 architecture, 9 painting
performing art: [ballet], 3 dance, 6 theatre, 10 opera   (10 marks)

18.2
1 throw	4 setting	7 abstract	9 plot
2 extracts	5 portrait	8 critics	10 e-books
3 series	6 art		(10 marks)

18.3
1 works of art / art	3 arts	5 arts and crafts
2 art lovers	4 art	6 fine arts (6 marks)

18.4
1 reproduction	4 literary	7 artistic
2 sculptor	5 character	8 bestseller
3 review	6 passage	9 architect (9 marks)

Test 19

19.1
1 cast	3 venue	5 costumes	7 dialogue	9 audience
2 stage	4 sets	6 set	8 direction	10 review (10 marks)

19.2
1 h	3 f	5 i	7 c	9 j
2 k	4 a	6 b	8 g	10 e (10 marks)

19.3
1 c	3 a	5 h	7 b	9 e
2 f	4 j	6 k	8 d	10 i (10 marks)

19.4   1 Correct
2 Correct, but *Katie is very enthusiastic about the theatre* is also possible.
3 Incorrect. *Do come to <u>the</u> cinema with us this evening!*
4 Correct, but *What made you so interested in the ballet?* is also possible.
5 Incorrect. *My parents took me to <u>the</u> opera on Saturday.*   (5 marks)

Test 20

20.1
1 My tastes ~~of~~ *in* music are very different from my parents'.
2 I loved the ~~musics~~ *music* they played at the concert, didn't you?
3 Nathan is a very talented ~~base~~ *bass* guitarist.
4 Helena can't read music but she's very good at playing ~~on~~ *by* ear.
5 Marek only needs to hear a tune once to be able to pick it ~~off~~ *out* on the piano.
6 Which do you prefer – pop or ~~classic~~ *classical* music?
7 What do you think of the ~~leader~~ *lead* singer in the band?
8 I'm not really ~~onto~~ *into* folk music.
9 Every culture has its own traditional ways of ~~doing~~ *making* music.
10 An album is made up of a number of individual ~~tricks~~ *tracks*. (10 marks)

20.2 1 hip hop 2 jazz 3 classical 4 r and b 5 rap (5 marks)

20.3
| 1 canned | 3 stream | 5 read | 7 composed | 9 become |
| 2 sync | 4 trained | 6 tune | 8 has | 10 taste | (10 marks)

20.4
1 Correct
2 Incorrect – a bass guitar plays the lowest range of notes.
3 Incorrect – 60s music is music from the 1960s
4 Incorrect – a list of music on your MP3 player or computer
5 Correct
6 Incorrect – a type of musical instrument
7 Incorrect – short for *synchronise*
8 Incorrect – music from a film or TV show
9 Correct
10 Correct (10 marks)

Test 21

21.1

	same	different
1	both are types of menu in a restaurant	*a set menu* is a limited selection of dishes at a fixed price; *à la carte* is a longer list of individual dishes
2	both are ways of describing food that needs more time to be ready	*unripe* is used to describe fruit that has not become sweet and tasty; *underdone* is used to describe food that has not been cooked enough
3	both are ways of describing a curry	*hot* = spicy, with lots of strong spices; *mild* = not very spicy, not a lot of pepper
4	both are put on a table laid for a meal	*cutlery* is made of metal (knives, forks and spoons) and *napkins* are made of cloth or paper (to protect your clothes when you are eating)
5	both do not eat certain kinds of food	a *vegetarian* doesn't eat meat or fish (and some don't eat eggs or cheese); a *non-meat eater* just doesn't eat meat

(10 marks)

21.2
| 1 h | 3 a | 5 b | 7 e | 9 k |
| 2 j | 4 c | 6 i | 8 f | 10 g | (10 marks)

21.3 1 N 2 N 3 P 4 P 5 P 6 N (6 marks)

21.4
| 1 afters | 3 cancel | 5 refill; when | 7 specials |
| 2 Organic | 4 help | 6 dishes | 8 season | (9 marks)

Test 22

22.1
| 1 plain | 3 glacier | 5 gorge | 7 summit | 9 source |
| 2 geyser | 4 peninsula | 6 mouth | 8 tributary | 10 stream | (10 marks)

22.2
1 *the* Himalayas
2 – Russia
3 *the* United States
4 – Lake Baikal
5 *the* Amazon

6 – Australia
7 – Mount Kilimanjaro
8 *the* West Indies
9 *the* Caribbean
10 *the* Straits of Gibraltar

(10 marks)

22.3 **Where land meets sea:** [bay], coast, gulf, shore, cliff
Part of mountain: foot, peak, ridge
Part of river: waterfall, delta, estuary

(10 marks)

22.4 thermal springs; ice fields; active volcano; the country's ageing population;
the area's most profitable crops

(5 marks)

Test 23

23.1
1 greenhouse effect
2 carbon footprint
3 fossil fuels
4 global warming
5 climate change

6 acid rain
7 polar ice cap
8 endangered species
9 air pollution
10 ozone depletion

(10 marks)

23.2 These are the most likely answers. However, there are also some other possibilities
e.g. *indestructible* for (1) or *dangerous* for (15). Check with a dictionary or your
teacher if you think you have come up with a correct answer that is not given below.

1 destructive
2 destructively
3 disposal
4 disposable

5 environmentalist
6 environmental
7 environmentally
8 globalise

9 global
10 globally
11 pollution
12 pollutant

13 polluted
14 endanger
15 endangered
16 ecological

(16 marks)

23.3
1 air pollution, a kind of fog found in cities and caused by smoke, chemicals and gases
2 distinct types
3 place which offers special protection to wildlife
4 catching fish in too large numbers
5 no longer in existence, having completely died out
6 environmental
7 thrown away after use
8 reuse rather than dispose of
9 all over the world, globally

(9 marks)

Test 24

24.1
1 swimming pool
2 art gallery
3 opera house

4 radio station
5 registry office
6 department store

7 law court(s)
8 taxi rank

9 skating rink
10 golf course

(10 marks)

24.2
1 police station. A *police station* is the place where the police work; the others are all places
where people pay for overnight accommodation.
2 garden centre. A *garden centre* is a kind of shop; the others are places offering people
advice / help.
3 suburbs. *Suburbs* relates to districts of a town; the others are all problems found
in urban areas.
4 filthy. *Filthy* is a negative adjective; the others are all positive.
5 chemist's. A *chemist's* is a kind of shop; the others are all places of culture /
entertainment.

(10 marks)

24.3
1 population
2 liveliest
3 cultural

4 adventurous
5 historic
6 residential

7 spacious
8 buildings
9 vandalism

(9 marks)

| 24.4 | 1 d | 2 g | 3 e | 4 a | 5 c | 6 b | (6 marks) |

Test 25

25.1
1 hoof	4 beak	7 trunk (of tree)	9 bud
2 snail	5 branch	8 worm	10 frog
3 bat	6 nest			(10 marks)

25.2
1 pollen	4 paws	7 fur	9 petals
2 peacock	5 wings	8 shark	10 tail
3 roots	6 bark			(10 marks)

25.3
| 1 breed | 3 grow | 5 blossom |
| 2 pick up | 4 lay | 6 pick | (6 marks) |

25.4
| 1 twigs | 3 breed | 5 pigeon | 7 owls | 9 hoof |
| 2 claws | 4 whale | 6 bough | 8 whiskers | (9 marks) |

Test 26

26.1
1 coat	4 pyjamas	7 helmet	9 slippers
2 cuff	5 sleeve	8 cardigan	10 zip
3 buckle	6 collar			(10 marks)

26.2
1 out	4 out	7 on	9 of
2 of	5 down	8 out	10 up
3 up	6 in			(10 marks)

26.3
| 1 f | 2 d | 3 a | 4 e | 5 b | (5 marks) |

26.4
1 inside out	4 national	7 heels	9 badge
2 suits	5 casually	8 disguise	10 laces
3 elegant	6 mask			(10 marks)

Test 27

27.1
1 temperature	4 bruises	7 breathless	9 pain
2 operation	5 indigestion	8 lump	10 injection
3 bandage	6 virus			(10 marks)

27.2
1 c	4 a	7 j	9 h
2 g	5 i	8 e	10 f
3 k	6 d			(10 marks)

27.3
1 voice	4 exhausted	7 tremble	9 rash
2 dislocate	5 contract	8 dizzy	10 shiver
3 infection	6 itches			(10 marks)

27.4 black eye; sore throat; blood pressure; chest pains; earache   (5 marks)

Test 28

28.1
1 manufactured	4 provide	7 operate	9 correct
2 describe	5 diagnose	8 use	10 wear
3 connected	6 treat			(10 marks)

28.2
| 1 crutches | 3 contact lenses | 5 scanner |
| 2 X-ray | 4 wheelchair | 6 hearing aid | (6 marks) |

28.3
1 general; operation
2 spectacles; vision
3 pacemaker; device
4 Keyhole
5 artificial
6 vast; difficulties
7 databases; tool
8 advances; decade
9 highly
10 lenses; aid
11 pressure; automatically

(19 marks)

Test 29

29.1
1 harmful
2 lowering
3 sharp
4 processed
5 boost; immune
6 exercise
7 source
8 short-term; process

(10 marks)

29.2

1 False	4 False	7 True	10 False
2 True	5 True	8 False	11 True
3 False	6 False	9 False	12 False

(12 marks)

29.3
1 *To maintain your fitness* means *to keep your fitness at the same level*.
3 *Wholemeal bread* is bread made from whole flour that has had nothing removed.
4 A *major* problem is a *significant* problem.
6 A label showing the salt content of a food states how much salt there is in it.
8 We say that bad habits like smoking *cause* harm to the body.
9 *Superfoods* are foods that are particularly good for the health.
10 If you are *under stress* at work, it means that things are difficult for you there.
12 *Fit* is an adjective meaning *healthy* or *in good physical condition*. (8 marks)

29.4
1 fruits   2 fruit   3 foods   4 food   5 foods   (5 marks)

Test 30

30.1
1 platform. *Cockpit*, *wings* and *aisle* are parts of a plane; *platform* is part of a railway station.
2 deck. *Ticket collector*, *steward* and *captain* are all people; *deck* is part of a ship.
3 breakdown service. *Terminal*, *port* and *petrol station* are all places; a *breakdown service* is a kind of service.
4 motorist. *Air traffic controller*, *ground staff* and *cabin crew* are all people whose work is connected with flying; a *motorist* is someone who drives a car.
5 ferry. *High speed train*, *buffet* and *express* are all connected with rail transport; a *ferry* is a kind of boat.

(10 marks – 1 for identifying the odd one out and 1 for giving an appropriate reason)

30.2

Z	H	B	T	E	R	T	C	I	L
V	E	L	R	A	D	U	K	O	I
S	L	V	A	N	X	Y	P	L	M
H	I	O	M	R	O	A	Y	I	N
I	C	O	N	D	U	C	T	O	R
B	O	O	T	V	C	H	L	O	P
M	P	U	N	C	A	T	N	U	R
A	T	E	S	X	B	Y	T	U	K
W	E	X	H	A	I	H	G	I	M
E	R	Q	G	A	N	G	W	A	Y
T	C	H	A	U	F	F	E	U	R

(8 marks)

30.3
1 delayed
2 jetlag
3 seasickness
4 a voyage
5 runway
6 a duty-free shop
7 bumpy
8 to be on standby
9 a cruise
10 a seat reservation
11 put someone up
12 on time
(12 marks)

30.4
1 travel   2 run   3 journey   4 trip   5 get   (5 marks)

Test 31

31.1
1 package holiday
2 cruise
3 self-catering
4 campsite
5 youth hostel
6 excursion
7 guesthouse
8 caravan
9 holiday brochure
10 adventure holiday
(10 marks)

31.2
1 i   3 h   5 j   7 k   9 d
2 g   4 a   6 b   8 e   10 c   (10 marks)

31.3
1 a winding road
2 an exclusive night-club
3 picturesque charm
4 a breathtaking climb
5 a fascinating museum
6 exceptional food
7 a luxurious lifestyle
8 a unique opportunity
9 a memorable holiday
10 surrounding countryside
(10 marks)

31.4
1 glamorise
2 inconveniently
3 exhilaration
4 luxurious
5 memorable
(5 marks)

Test 32

32.1
1 rotate
2 utilise
3 extract
4 flash
5 analyse
6 combine
7 insert
8 experiment
9 install
10 dissect
(10 marks)

32.2
1 engineering
2 molecular
3 enables
4 creation
5 genetically
6 traditional
(6 marks)

32.3
1 satnav
2 HD camcorder
3 tablet
4 digital photo frame
5 smartphone
(5 marks)

32.4
1 soil
2 organs
3 flaw; theory
4 chemicals; reacted
5 Ergonomics; space
6 lever
7 alter; DNA
8 branches
9 structure; cells
(14 marks)

Test 33

33.1
1 gigabyte
2 laptop
3 display
4 spreadsheet
5 cursor
6 software
7 database
8 graphics
9 device
10 network
(10 marks)

33.2
1 False
2 True
3 False
4 True
5 False
6 False
7 True
8 False
9 True
10 True
(10 marks)

33.3
1 A virus causes problems for your computer
3 *RAM* stands for *random access memory*.
5 A scanner lets you transfer pictures and text into a computer.
6 A tablet is usually operated by a touch screen.
8 *PC* stands for *personal computer*.
(5 marks)

33.4
1 delete
2 back up; crashed
3 upgrade
4 download
5 key in
6 click
7 store
8 Plug
9 undo
(10 marks)

Test 34

34.1
1 attach	4 Skype	7 access
2 enter	5 down	8 in; subscribe
3 browse	6 Google	9 keep (10 marks)

34.2 social networking; bookmark; service provider; username; password; broadband; contact list; online gaming; virtual reality; home page (10 marks)

34.3 1 f   2 d   3 a   4 b   5 c   6 e   (6 marks)

34.4
1 engine	4 on / in	7 hits
2 provider	5 attachment	8 webcam
3 wiki	6 out / off	9 questions (9 marks)

Test 35

35.1
1 Many of the articles in ~~tablet~~ *tabloid* newspapers are about TV and pop stars.
2 *Neighbours* is a popular Australian ~~soup~~ *soap*.
3 That magazine publishes some very good ~~in-deep~~ *in-depth* articles about the economy.
4 Satellite ~~discs~~ *dishes* are useful but can look very ugly on the sides of houses.
5 Popular newspapers are more interested in ~~sensitivity~~ *sensation* than real news.
6 Which is your preferred ~~mean~~ *means* of communication?
7 My cousin has just got a great job as a ~~present~~ *presenter* on a TV breakfast show.
8 John loves watching programmes about ~~currency~~ *current* affairs.
9 Serious newspapers are also sometimes referred to as ~~quantity~~ *quality* papers.
10 I hate it when a good film on TV is constantly interrupted by ~~commercialists~~ *commercials*. (10 marks)

35.2
1 dubbed	6 televise
2 receive	7 stream
3 subscribed	8 investigating
4 is	9 focused (other tenses possible here too)
5 were tweeting (other tenses possible here too)	10 was shot (10 marks)

35.3
1 talk show	6 sports show
2 game show	7 wildlife documentary
3 weather forecast	8 detective drama
4 soap	9 sitcom
5 cartoon	10 current affairs programme (10 marks)

35.4 1 showing   2 subscription   3 podcasts   4 mass   5 episode   (5 marks)

Test 36

36.1
1 cast; politician; polling	3 stand; seat	5 chamber
2 head	4 nominate; judge	6 legislature (10 marks)

36.2 US: Congress, Senate, President, representative, House of Representatives
UK: [House of Lords], Prime Minister, monarch, MP, Parliament, House of Commons (10 marks)

36.3
1 to select	3 a ballot paper	5 a republic
2 to head	4 his or her term of office	(5 marks)

36.4
1 Independence	5 monarchy	8 politically
2 election	6 federation	9 government
3 policies	7 dictatorship	10 presidential
4 majority		(10 marks)

Test 37

37.1
1 offence	4 deliberations	7 victim	9 accomplice
2 tried	5 innocent	8 case	10 proof
3 prosecuting	6 punishment		(10 marks)

37.2
| 1 shoplifting | 3 kidnapping | 5 burglary |
| 2 murder | 4 terrorism | 6 smuggling | (6 marks) |

37.3
1 robbed	5 court	9 verdict	12 served
2 stole	6 trial	10 sentenced	13 released
3 arrested	7 pleaded	11 prison	14 time
4 charged	8 evidence		(14 marks)

37.4
1 The police sus<u>pect</u>ed Sarah of stealing the money.
2 The <u>con</u>victs were set to work in the mines.
3 Paul was asked a lot of questions about the crime but is not a <u>suspect</u>.
4 The police are hopeful that the accused will be con<u>vict</u>ed.
5 The man I told the police about is now their main <u>suspect</u>. (5 words)   (5 marks)

Test 38

38.1
| 1 salaries | 3 outgoings | 5 charges | 7 mortgage | 9 debit |
| 2 pay | 4 overdrawn | 6 loan | 8 deposit | 10 cash | (10 marks) |

38.2
1 *Income* is money coming into an account; *outgoings* are money going out of an account.
2 *Inheritance tax* is tax on what a person leaves after their death; *corporation tax* is a tax on business.
3 A *current account* is one used for daily income and expenditure; a *savings account* is one used for saving money (money is in it for longer and it earns interest).
4 A *debt* is money owed to someone; a *payment* is money paid to someone.
(8 marks – 2 marks for each question)

38.3
1 tax	4 rates	7 raise	10 facility
2 duty	5 financing	8 excise	11 transfer
3 open	6 credit	9 combine	12 steady	(12 marks)

38.4   1 competitive   2 repayments   3 banking   4 overdraft   5 expenses   (5 marks)

Test 39

39.1 conventional – bizarre; transparent – opaque; natural – artificial; strong – weak; genuine – fake; decorative – plain; faulty – perfect; stiff – flexible; vivid – sombre; delicate – tough   (10 marks)

39.2

adjective	noun
entire	[entirety]
solid	*solidity*
decent	decency
precise	*precision*
characteristic	character
severe	*severity*
trivial	triviality

(6 marks)

39.3
1 flexible	5 plain	8 sturdy	11 decent
2 precise	6 fragile	9 vivid	12 entire
3 trivial	7 faulty	10 characteristic	13 bizarre
4 an artificial			(13 marks)

39.4 1 The writer's latest book isn't half as interesting as her first one. OR The writer's first book isn't half as interesting as her latest one.
2 It's a reasonably good hotel, in my opinion.
3 Andy has got a great big bruise on his leg.
4 My father likes his tea unusually strong.
5 Hilly's motorbike is nowhere near as powerful as her boyfriend's.
6 We have a lot of pretty thick books to read for our course.   (6 marks)

Test 40

40.1
1 e	3 f	5 k	7 i	9 d
2 c	4 g	6 h	8 j	10 a	(10 marks)

40.2 traditional – conservative; middle-of-the-road – moderate; dedicated – committed; eccentric – odd; radical – extreme   (5 marks)

40.3
1 against	4 on (*about* is also possible)	7 in; of
2 of	5 of	8 to
3 in	6 about	9 In	(10 marks)

40.4
1 a pacifist	5 conservative	9 intellectual
2 a vegetarian / non-meat eater	6 left-wing	10 personal
3 a socialist	7 moderate views	
4 a Muslim	8 moral values, morals	(10 marks)

Test 41

41.1
1 F	3 T	5 T	7 F	9 F
2 T	4 F	6 T	8 T	10 T	(10 marks)

41.2
1 inspired	3 discontented	5 confused
2 furious	4 content	(5 marks)

41.3
1 rather depressed	5 rather grateful	9 totally thrilled
2 totally delighted	6 rather inspired	10 rather upset
3 rather enthusiastic	7 rather nervous	
4 totally furious	8 totally sick and tired	(10 marks)

41.4
1 anxious	5 thrilled / thrilling	9 confused / confusing
2 enthusiastic	6 depressed / depressing	10 nervous
3 grateful	7 furious	
4 inspired / inspiring	8 thankful	(10 marks)

Test 42

42.1 1 His behaviour appals me.
2 It's been so difficult at work. I'm longing for my holiday.
3 Maria is very fond of romantic novels.
4 Amy didn't find Ben attractive.
5 He cares more for / about his daughter than anyone else in the world.
6 I can't bear standing in queues.
7 Violent films disgust me.
8 I always dread the thought of going back to work after a holiday.
9 His enthusiasm and energy appeal to me.
10 Paddy can't stand his new boss.   (10 marks)

42.2
1 in	4 for / about	7 forward	9 for
2 with	5 to	8 to	10 on
3 by	6 about		(10 marks)

42.3   All the statements are false.   (5 marks)

42.4   1 Marxists are passionate about *the work of Karl Marx.*
2 Sadists *enjoy* causing pain.
3 Claustrophobics can't stand *feeling enclosed.*
4 Ornithologists are fascinated by *birds.*
5 Misogynists can't stand *any women.*   (5 marks)

42.5   **liking:** [desire], fascinated, yearn, affectionate
disliking: repel, revolt   (5 marks)

Test 43

43.1

1 threatened	4 insisted	7 complained	9 grumbled
2 stuttered	5 confessed	8 begged	10 urged
3 boasted	6 murmured		(10 marks)

43.2

1 he said furiously.	5 said guiltily.	9 said the child crossly.
2 said Bob nervously.	6 said softly	10 said the boy's mother encouragingly.
3 said proudly.	7 said angrily.	
4 said firmly.	8 said desperately.	(10 marks)

43.3   1 My aunt insisted *on buying* me a present.
2 I really object *to* people *smoking* in my house.
3 They are always grumbling *about having* to work on Sundays.
4 The accused has never confessed *to committing* the murder.
5 He begged me *for* money and then begged me *to help* him find somewhere to live.
6 Mark complained *to* his boss *about* his colleague *getting* the sack.
7 Jo has threatened *to make* an official complaint *to* her boss if things don't improve.
8 Harriet is always arguing *with* her parents *about tidying* her room.
9 Will Brad ever stop boasting *about winning* first prize.   (9 marks)

43.4   1 sad   2 angry   3 sad   4 happy   5 angry   6 happy   (6 marks)

Test 44

44.1   **sight:** [gaze], glimpse, witness; **hearing:** deafening, silent; **taste:** [mild] salty, spicy;
touch: poke, tap; **smell:** putrid, stinking   (10 marks)

44.2

1 observe	3 pat	5 handle	7 grab	9 peered
2 staring	4 press	6 glanced	8 Poke; notice	10 grasp (11 marks)

44.3   1 b   2 a   3 e   4 d   (4 marks)

44.4

1 tastes too mild.	5 looks wonderful.	8 smells so fragrant.
2 looks fat.	6 sounds very pleasant.	9 smells musty.
3 looks rather green.	7 feels so soft.	10 tastes too sweet.
4 sounds very exciting.		(10 marks)

Test 45

45.1

1 c	3 k	5 a	7 j	9 e
2 h	4 f	6 b	8 d	10 g (10 marks)

45.2   1 rumble. All the actions except *rumble* are done by the mouth.
2 sigh. All the actions except *sigh* are done by the whole body.
3 blush. All the actions except *blush* are done by the eyes.
4 grin. All the actions except *grin* are connected with having a cold.
5 sweat. All the actions except *sweat* make a noise.   (10 marks – one for identifying the
odd one out and one for giving an
appropriate reason)

45.3 1 Drink this water to help you swallow the pill (10).
2 Having had so little sleep last night, he's been yawning all day (4).
3 If you chew your food well, you digest it more easily (2).
4 She's frowning because her children are behaving so badly (Example).
5 Some people sneeze if they come into contact with a cat (6).
6 She sighed with relief when she heard that Nick had arrived safely (8).
7 Try blinking to see if you can get the dust out of your eye (3).
8 You can tell that he's nervous because his hands are trembling (1).
9 She always blushes whenever she's embarrassed (7).
10 Take a couple of deep breaths and you won't feel so nervous (5).   (10 marks)

45.4 1 to breathe   2 bit, bitten   3 a grin   4 shook, shaken   5 perspiration   (5 marks)

Test 46

46.1 **praising:** on the ball, out of this world, streets ahead, top-notch, have a way with
criticising: [at fault], pick holes in, run down, take the biscuit, want
to have your cake and eat it, to blame   (10 marks)

46.2 1 Emma is head and ~~neck~~ *shoulders* above the other pupils at French.
2 Markus is a great gardener – he truly has ~~colourful~~ *green* fingers.
3 They say that people from that part of the world have the gift of the ~~gabble~~ *gab*.
4 Toby has a very high opinion of himself; he thinks he's the cat's ~~paws~~ *whiskers*.
5 The film was absolutely first-~~mark~~ *rate* / first-*class* – totally absorbing.
6 I can't understand why Becky thinks she's the bee's ~~stripes~~ *knees*.
7 When it comes to punctuation, I'm the world's ~~worse~~ *worst*.
8 My little boy is ~~along~~ *among* the best in his class at reading.
9 Tanya's ~~kilometres~~ *miles* better than me at swimming.
10 It was annoying to have to pay for the repairs to our car after the accident
when we were not ~~with~~ *at* fault.   (10 marks)

46.3 1 giving opinion   3 serious   5 serious   7 important
2 important   4 not pleased   6 giving opinion   8 not pleased   (8 marks)

46.4 1 totally   3 brilliantly   5 picking   7 streets
2 for   4 highly   6 cake   (7 marks)

Test 47

47.1 1 P   3 N   5 P   7 P   9 N
2 N   4 P   6 N   8 P   10 P   (10 marks)

47.2 1 bear   3 stiff   5 long   7 cool   9 swelled
2 door   4 shoes   6 wobbly   8 chin   10 life   (10 marks)

47.3 1 i   3 h   5 a   7 c   9 g
2 j   4 k   6 b   8 f   10 e   (10 marks)

47.4 1 Fatima's feeling under the weather.
2 Mona throws a wobbly if she doesn't get her own way.
3 Ian is doing his best to keep his chin up.
4 All the children are in high spirits.
5 The children were scared out of their wits.   (5 marks)

Test 48

48.1 1 the hatchet   5 under the carpet   9 our act together
2 a dead end   6 the bottom of things   10 a turning point
3 a grasp   7 the end of the tunnel   (10 marks)
4 take notice   8 The tide

48.2
1 It must be dreadful to be deprived ~~from~~ *of* your freedom.
2 I'm ~~on~~ *in* a bit of a dilemma at the moment.
3 I can't face the thought ~~about~~ *of* leaving this town.
4 I think we should all lay our cards ~~over~~ *on* the table.
5 I hope everyone will sit ~~down~~ *up* and take notice.
6 We need to do our utmost to get ~~at~~ *to* the bottom of things.
7 Josh has been telling me about the fix he's ~~at~~ *in*.
8 I thought we were making progress but now we seem to have come ~~at~~ *to* a dead end.
9 It's usually better not to try to sweep things ~~below~~ *under* the carpet. (9 marks)

48.3
1 disaster	3 broken	5 lacks	7 challenges	9 muddle	
2 stirring	4 affected	6 mildly	8 take	10 facing	(10 marks)

48.4

verb	affect	annoy	irritate	*collapse*	disrupt	*lack*	deprive
noun	[effect]	*annoyance*	*irritation / irritant*	collapse	*disruption*	lack	*deprivation*

(6 marks)

Test 49

49.1
little: minute, a drop, tiny
big: [heaps], enormous, tons, gigantic, loads, significant, substantial, vast (10 marks)

49.2
1 tons	5 drop / dash	9 scores
2 considerable	6 average	10 total
3 excessive	7 significant / substantial	
4 dozens	8 loads	(10 marks)

49.3
1 disbelief	4 inadequate	7 ban	9 impossible
2 chaos	5 unacceptable	8 dependent	10 unexpected
3 different	6 nonsense		(10 marks)

49.4
1 heaps	2 loads	3 scores	4 tons	5 bags	(5 marks)

Test 50

50.1
2 circle	5 circumference	8 octagon	10 triangle
3 diameter	6 pentagon	9 spiral	11 angle
4 radius	7 rectangle		(10 marks)

50.2
1 twenty-five degrees Centigrade / Celsius
2 three squared
3 six point eight
4 The room is five metres by seven metres.
5 nine tenths
6 six cubed
7 forty-one per cent
8 nine to the power of seven
9 two million, three hundred and fifty-two thousand, seven hundred and ninety-six
10 two x plus six y (10 marks)

50.3
1 circular	4 triangular	7 division	9 addition
2 spherical	5 oval	8 octagonal	10 cubic / cubed
3 multiply	6 spiral		(10 marks)

50.4
1 semicircle
2 hemisphere
3 minus
4 oh / zero (less standard)
5 sides / corners / angles (5 marks)

Test 51

51.1
1 True	3 False	5 False	7 False	9 False
2 False	4 True	6 False	8 True	10 True	(10 marks)

51.2   2 It ~~lasts~~ *takes* ten hours to fly from Tokyo to Rome.
3 The verb *elapse* is used mainly in the present perfect, past perfect or past simple.
5 We say: This DVD will ~~go~~ *last* or *run* for two and a half hours.
6 It means: *Time passes more quickly when you're enjoying yourself.*
7 *The train arrived on time* means the train arrived punctually.
9 *The meeting dragged on for two hours* suggests that the speaker
found the meeting boring.   (6 marks)

51.3
1 just in time	5 at a time
2 time and time again	6 at times; from time to time
3 on time	7 By the time
4 for the time being	8 for a time (9 marks)

51.4
1 Ages	4 spells	7 an era	9 stages
2 spell	5 age	8 phase	10 fleeting
3 timeless	6 momentary		(10 marks)

Test 52

52.1

adjective	verb	noun
long	[lengthen]	*length*
short	*shorten*	
wide	*widen*	*width*
deep	*deepen*	*depth*
broad	*broaden*	*breadth*
high	*heighten*	*height*

(10 marks)

52.2
1 broaden	4 width	7 shortened	9 breadth
2 depth	5 lengths	8 widen	10 height
3 heightened	6 deepened		(10 marks)

52.3   1 The economy expanded very rapidly last year.
2 We are planning to extend our house.
3 This shirt shrank when I washed it.
4 New houses have spread / are spreading into the countryside. (*Spread* is a dynamic verb so *into* is better than *in* here.)
5 The national park stretches as far as the eye can see / across all the area you can see.   (5 marks)

52.4
1 high	4 faraway	7 shallow	9 broad
2 taller	5 broad-minded	8 wide	10 long
3 distant	6 raised		(10 marks)

Test 53

53.1
1 compulsory	4 optional	7 forced	9 choice
2 obliged	5 exempt	8 liable	10 obligatory
3 mandatory	6 alternative		(10 words)

53.2   1 The country had a shortage of engineers so a foreign company built the road.
2 The astronaut died through lack of oxygen.
3 When I got home after being away the lawn was in need of mowing.
4 There is a need for more discussion before we can make a decision.
5 The garden wants watering / wants water before we put the new flowers in.   (5 marks)

53.3
1 without   4 no; but   7 of   9 for
2 for   5 from   8 through; of   10 whether
3 in; of   6 is; to   (14 marks)

53.4
1 doubtful   3 opportunity   5 probable; certainty
2 chance   4 inevitable   (6 marks)

Test 54

54.1

(bang S)	chime S	flash L	flicker L	glow L	hiss S
hum S	rustle S	shine L	thud S	twinkle L	

(10 marks)

54.2
1 noise   4 beam   7 rumble   9 gloomy
2 glowing   5 crashing   8 twinkling   10 racket
3 screeched   6 dim   (10 marks)

54.3
1 c   2 i   3 a   4 g   5 d   6 h   7 b   8 e   (8 marks)

54.4
1 sparkling; glittering   3 rattled   5 flickered
2 chiming   4 hum   6 rays   (7 marks)

Test 55

55.1
1 landlord; landlady   4 donate   7 estate
2 tenant   5 proprietor   8 belongings
3 possessions   6 inherit   9 sponsor   (10 marks)

55.2
1 of   3 for   5 out   7 for
2 away   4 over   6 with   8 with   (8 marks)

55.3
1 hand over   4 was left   7 provide   9 sponsor
2 donate   5 support   8 handed down   10 allocated
3 present   6 cater   (10 marks)

55.4
1 allocated   4 left   7 giving out
2 go   5 present
3 supported   6 properties   (7 marks)

Test 56

56.1
1 The river flowed through the valley.
2 The car drove away at high speed with two passengers in it.
3 The ferry sailed across the Channel.
4 The train travelled at high speed along the new track.
5 The clouds drifted across the sky.
6 The flag fluttered in the light wind.
7 The leaves began to stir in the gentle breeze.
8 The trees swayed in the strong wind.
9 The lorry had to swerve to avoid a cat.
10 The children dawdled along the road towards school.   (10 marks)

56.2

verb	past simple
dawdle [S]	[dawdled]
hurry F	hurried
crawl S	crawled
tear F	tore
shoot F	shot
creep S	crept
plod S	plodded

(12 marks)

56.3 1 velocity 2 rate 3 speed 4 pace 5 pace 6 rate (6 marks)

56.4 1 speed 4 plodded 6 dawdling
2 sail 5 tore 7 swaying (7 marks)
3 move

Test 57

57.1 1 e 3 g 5 j 7 k 9 a
2 i 4 b 6 h 8 c 10 d (10 marks)

57.2 1 shady 4 bulky 7 feather 9 polished
2 dazzling 5 sleek / silky 8 lead 10 hollow
3 prickly 6 jagged (10 marks)

57.3 heavy / light suitcase; solid / hollow bricks; dull / vivid colours; dense / sparse vegetation;
thick / fine hair (10 marks)

57.4 1 feel 2 underfoot 3 surface 4 touch 5 glare (5 marks)

Test 58

58.1

verb	noun	adjective
accomplish	[accomplishment]	*accomplished*
succeed	*success*	*successful*
attain	*attainment*	*attainable*
harden	*hardness*	hard
fulfil	*fulfilment*	*fulfilling*
	difficulty	difficult

(10 marks)

58.2 1 We managed to finish 5 achieved its targets
2 I can manage ten kilometres 6 succeeded in persuading / managed to persuade
3 has accomplished a great deal 7 has been having considerable success
4 her plans will come off 8 had a lot of difficulty finding (8 marks)

58.3 1 attain – an ambition, a target 4 fulfil – an ambition, a dream, an obligation
2 secure – an agreement 5 achieve – an ambition, a dream, a target,
3 realise – an ambition, a dream a compromise (12 marks – 1 mark for each correct word)

58.4 1 to 2 in 3 with 4 under 5 with (5 marks)

Test 59

59.1 1 She was flying into Paris ~~in~~ *at* the very time that I was flying out.
2 I realised I'd left my keys on the kitchen table ~~as just~~ *just as* I closed the
front door.
3 *Prior to* taking up a position with Reynolds, Morris worked at CentreBank.
4 A new school library is currently under construction. ~~During~~ *In* the meantime
the children are using the City Library.
5 We'll deal with those issues ~~on~~ *at* a later stage in the project.
6 I was home by midday but I had to go out earlier ~~in~~ *on*.
7 Katy's moving to London in September but *meanwhile / in the meantime* she's
living with us.

8 I'll have to repair the fence ~~on~~ *at* some point but it's not too urgent.
9 *Following* ~~of~~ my holiday job in a hospital, I decided to train as a nurse.
10 I last saw Peter at Maria's wedding. ~~In~~ *On that occasion* he was unusually friendly towards me.

(10 marks)

59.2 **before:** earlier on, formerly, previously, prior
after: [later], following, thereafter, subsequently
at the same time: simultaneously, the very moment

(9 marks)

59.3 1 In a) it is clear that the speaker's parents lived in Cambridge for the entire period of the war. In b) it is not clear exactly how long they lived in Cambridge; they may have been there for part of the war or for all of it.
2 In a) we know that Sally arrived at the exact moment when the speaker was going out of the door. In b) it is less precise – she might have arrived ten minutes or so before the speaker actually left.
3 In a) the writer worked on the novel and thought about the film script at the same time. In b) the writer did not think about the film script until after completing the novel.
4 In a) the reference is to the city's previous name. The sentence comes from a text written after 1991 when Leningrad once again became St Petersburg. In b) the sentence is talking about the city's later name. It probably comes from a text describing the city during the period before 1924, i.e. the date when the city was renamed Leningrad.

(8 marks)

59.4
1 immediate	3 The	5 some; during
2 just	4 Previously	6 occasions; thereafter

(8 marks)

Test 60

60.1 1 In the event of fire, use the staircase rather than the lift.
2 What if you don't get the work finished on time; is that going to be a major problem?
3 You can get up whenever you like / want tomorrow.
4 You cannot enter the country unless you have a visa
5 Take a warm coat with you in case it gets cold in the evenings.
6 No matter what happens, I'll always love you.
7 You can stay with us as long as you like on condition (that) you help out with the housework.
8 Under no circumstances would I agree to move house again. OR I wouldn't agree to move house again under any circumstances.
9 It's going to take a long time to get there, whichever route you take.
10 You can join the tennis club as / so long as you're over 16.

(10 marks)

60.2 1 Skype makes it easier to keep in touch with family ~~whoever~~ *wherever* they are in the world.
2 Make sure you have your mobile phone with you ~~in the case of~~ *in case you have / there is* an emergency.
3 What ~~about~~ *if* we don't have enough money to pay for the meal, what'll happen then?
4 Take your driving licence with you in case you ~~will decide~~ *decide* to hire a car.
5 I wouldn't share a flat with her under ~~no~~ *any* circumstances. OR *Under no circumstances would I* share a flat with her.

(10 marks – 1 for underlining each error and 1 for correcting it)

60.3
1 requirements	3 circumstances	5 prerequisite
2 conditions	4 event	

(5 marks)

60.4
1 how	4 that	7 on	9 case
2 Supposing	5 Under	8 Whoever	10 prerequisite
3 so	6 if		

(10 marks)

Test 61

61.1
1 to	4 to	7 of	9 on
2 about	5 of	8 as	10 in
3 from	6 for		

(10 marks)

61.2 **used to explain why something happened:** [aim], motive, grounds, purpose, reason
used to give the result of something that happened: consequence, outcome, upshot (7 marks)

61.3
1 The editor knew the article would spark (off) a lot of comment.
2 The shopping mall will generate a range of jobs for local people.
3 Owing to (the fact that there was) thick fog, our plane couldn't take off.
4 What caused Cathy to change her mind about handing in her notice?
5 Our problems stem from a misunderstanding.
6 What was the reason for Smith not being at today's meeting? OR What was the reason why Smith was not at today's meeting? OR What was the reason for Smith's absence from today's meeting?
7 The teacher explained the purpose of the activity to the class. OR The teacher explained to the class what the purpose of the activity was.
8 I never heard the upshot of the discussions.
9 The police are trying to discover Briggs's motive for stealing the file.
10 I suspect the Minister's speech will prompt an angry response. (10 marks)

61.4
1 Owing to *the fact that* the weather was bad, the open air concert was cancelled. OR *Owing to the bad weather*, the open air concert was cancelled.
2 I think her charm is the reason ~~of~~ *for* Juliet's success.
3 First, we have to deal with some matters ~~raising~~ *arising* from the last meeting.
4 Tim's talk ~~promoted~~ *provoked* a heated argument.
5 I left my purse at home and, ~~subsequently~~ *consequently*, had to walk back rather than get a bus.
6 We left the door open and, ~~for~~ *as* a result, the rain came in and soaked the carpet.
7 Let me start by explaining the purpose ~~from~~ *of* this project.
8 The match resulted ~~to~~ *in* a draw. (8 marks)

Test 62

62.1
1 accept	5 poles apart	9 a huge discrepancy
2 concede	6 Admittedly	10 the reverse was true
3 in contrast	7 That's all very well	
4 Although	8 acknowledged	(10 marks)

62.2
1 all very well	4 After all
2 reverse; true	5 world; difference
3 on; other hand	6 all that

(14 marks – 1 mark per word)

62.3
1 I concede (that) it's an interesting plan but it simply isn't practical.
2 The flat is pleasantly spacious but, on the other hand, it'd need a lot of decorating.
3 The two parties' environmental policies are poles apart.
4 At that time, there was a great divide between the lifestyles of the urban and rural classes. (4 marks)

62.4 yawning gap; it's all very well; poles apart; in contrast; after all; on the contrary; quite the opposite (7 marks)

Test 63

63.1 1 on; of   3 to   5 in; to   7 from
2 with   4 into   6 with   8 As   (10 marks)

63.2 1 He's very good-looking and, what's more, he's a nice person.
2 I help out with the housework and, in addition, do some cooking / in addition to doing some cooking. OR In addition to helping out with the housework, I do some cooking.
3 Jon can be very bad-tempered but, equally, his wife has a very sharp tongue.
4 They sell food, clothes, electrical goods and so on and so forth.
5 Further to your letter of 6 May, I am sending you the information you require.
6 It was cold and dark and, on top of (all) that, the baby was screaming.
7 Staff in this job need a knowledge of languages and, additionally, a driving licence.
8 Luke's a brilliant mathematician and a talented singer to boot.
9 Jennie came to the rehearsal along with two of her friends.
10 Your tennis would benefit from specialist coaching as well as more practice.   (10 marks)

63.3 1 *Alongside* ~~with~~ / *Along with* her own job, she also helps out her husband with his business.
2 Besides ~~they have~~ *having* a flat in London, they also own a cottage in the country.
3 We've got to paint the kitchen this weekend and tidy the garden ~~for~~ *to boot*.
4 In addition to ~~he speaks~~ *speaking* Russian, Tim knows a bit of Korean.
5 It's an interesting old town. ~~Furthermoreover~~ *Furthermore / Moreover*, it has a world-class university.
6 I feed the cats once a day, ~~or~~ *likewise* the dog.
7 We had to fill in a form, then have an interview, ~~and so forth and so on~~ *and so on and so forth*.
8 I need to get my passport renewed ~~and~~ *plus* I need to have some inoculations done.   (8 marks)

63.4 1 on top of all that   5 Apart from
2 Further to   6 and so on and so forth
3 into the bargain   7 Likewise
4 plus   (7 marks)

Test 64

64.1 **situation:** position, state of affairs
problem: crisis, difficulty
response: [approach] reaction, attitude
solution: answer, key
evaluation: assessment, judgement   (10 marks)

64.2 1 to   3 to   5 of   7 of
2 out; of   4 with; to   6 to   8 to   (10 marks)

64.3 1 point   3 question   5 argument
2 matters   4 aspect   (5 marks)

64.4 1 a fact   6 an approach
2 a reaction   7 an assessment
3 a claim   8 an issue
4 a solution   9 a state of affairs
5 a topic   10 an argument   (10 marks)

Test 65

65.1 1 Well then   4 Fine   7 for instance   9 b
2 Listen   5 Right   8 sort of   10 hold on
3 you know   6 I mean   (10 marks)

65.2
1 hang on	3 you see	5 mind you
2 now then	4 well then	(5 marks)

65.3
1 Mind you	f	6 like	a	
2 Look	b	7 Hang on	g	
3 Where was I?	k	8 Still	e	
4 Let me see	d	9 mean	i	
5 Anyway	j	10 a ; b	c	(20 marks – 1 for completing the phrase and
				1 for matching it to the correct comment)

Test 66

66.1
1 Turning to	6 Next
2 In conclusion	7 Thirdly
3 Briefly	8 Leaving aside
4 Secondly	9 In parenthesis
5 To sum up	10 Firstly (10 marks)

66.2 as it were – so to speak; finally – lastly; for instance – say; in conclusion – to conclude; in other words – that is to say; in summary – to sum up (6 marks)

66.3
1 True	4 False	7 False	10 False
2 False	5 False	8 True	11 False
3 False	6 True	9 False	(11 marks)

66.4
2 They have the same meaning but *that is to say* is more formal than *in other words*.
3 The preposition that follows *with reference* is *to*.
4 *It was stated **above*** can be used instead of *It was stated earlier*.
5 *Overleaf* means *on the other side of the page*.
7 They mean the same but *So to speak* is less formal.
9 *The table **below*** is used to mean the same as *the following table*.
10 An academic writer is more likely to say *See the tables in the appendix*.
11 *First of all* must always be written as three words. (8 marks)

Test 67

67.1
1 if you ask me	6 as luck would have it
2 as I was saying	7 as far as I'm concerned
3 come to think of it	8 that reminds me
4 if all else fails	9 if the worst comes to the worst
5 what with one thing and another	10 this, that and the other (10 marks)

67.2
1 f	3 i	5 c	7 k	9 b				
2 a	4 d	6 e	8 j	10 h	(10 marks)			

67.3
1 that	2 this; that	3 That	4 that	5 this	(6 marks)

67.4
1 far; concerned	3 have	5 with; another
2 comes	4 all; fails	6 ask (9 marks)

Test 68

68.1
1 long-winded; get to the point	5 small talk
2 talk shop	6 ball rolling
3 rubbish; sense; speak her mind	7 talk down
4 put it in a nutshell	(10 marks)

68.2
1 Reema could not understand James.
2 They were talking about two different things.

3 Marta misunderstood.
4 It's hard to say something because she talks so much.
5 It's not good to criticise someone in their absence.   (5 marks)

68.3 1 I think it's time to wrap ~~off~~ *up* the discussions, don't you?
2 The actor never imagined the film would become such a ~~speaking~~ *talking* point.
3 You can never get a word in ~~sideways~~ *edgeways* when Barry's around.
4 I'm afraid Megan's husband is not much good at ~~little~~ *small* talk.
5 So, who'd like to start the ball ~~moving~~ *rolling*?
6 To put it in a ~~nut~~ *nutshell*, the whole evening was a disaster.
7 Dad is inclined to get the wrong end of the ~~pole~~ *stick*.
8 I can't make ~~heads or tails~~ *head or tail* of Richard's book.   (16 marks – 1 for finding
each error and 1 for correcting it)

68.4 1 A: Joe won't have much time for his talk. B: Yes, he'll need to get to the point quickly.
2 A: Dan can be patronising, can't he? B: Yes, he does tend to talk down to people.
3 A: I wish Andrei weren't so long-winded. B: Yes, he loves the sound of his own voice.
4 A: You can rely on Ramzi to talk sense. B: Yes, he knows what he's talking about.
                                                                          (4 marks)

Test 69

69.1
1 sailor	4 shopper	7 supervisor	9 grater
2 sharpener	5 projector	8 hanger	10 donor
3 operator	6 employer		(10 marks)

69.2
1 excitement	4 admission	7 replacement	9 reduction
2 pollution	5 scarcity	8 complication	10 happiness
3 readiness	6 forgetfulness		(10 marks)

69.3
| 1 a pianist | 3 a physicist | 5 a cellist |
| 2 the addressee | 4 an employee | (5 marks) |

69.4
1 modernise	4 motherhood	7 friendship	9 unforgivable
2 beautify	5 outrageous	8 active	10 enjoyment
3 refusal	6 harmless		(10 marks)

Test 70

70.1
1 illegal	4 disapproves	7 irreplaceable	9 inedible
2 unwrapping	5 inexperienced	8 dislike	10 unlocking
3 illegible	6 impatient		(10 marks)

70.2
| 1 j | 3 i | 5 h | 7 b | 9 c | 11 d |
| 2 f | 4 k | 6 g | 8 e | 10 a | (11 marks) |

70.3 1 someone who used to be a soldier but no longer is
2 to be only partly literate, i.e. with very poor reading and writing skills
3 to read for a second time
4 to spell something incorrectly
5 to be in favour of the army
6 to give something too much emphasis
7 to put too low a value on something
8 to be against the government
9 something that you do without being conscious or aware of what you are doing
10 describing something that happens before a wedding, e.g. *pre-wedding nerves* (10 marks)

70.4
1 dissimilar. *Dissimilar* is an adjective and the other words are verbs.
2 ex-boss. In *ex-boss*, *ex* = *former* and in the other words it means *out of*.
3 unbend. *Unbend* is a verb and the other words are adjectives.
4 sensitive. In the negative form, the *in-* prefix doesn't change: *insensitive*; when the *in-* prefix is added to the other adjectives, it changes to double the base word's initial letter: *irrelevant, immoral, illiterate*. (4 marks)

Test 71

71.1
1 respect	4 prospect	7 support	9 reverted
2 educated	5 converts	8 produced	10 impressed
3 expresses	6 imposed		

(10 marks)

71.2
DUCT	lead
PONE, POSE	place, put
PORT	carry, take
SPECT	see, look
VERT	turn

(5 marks)

71.3
1 to import	4 to depress	7 to deport	9 to deposit
2 to conduct	5 to postpone	8 to inspect	10 to convert
3 to depose	6 to divert		

(10 marks)

71.4

verb	person noun	abstract noun
educate	[educator]	[education]
inspect	*inspector*	*inspection*
oppress	*oppressor*	*oppression*
compose	*composer*	*composition*
advertise	*advertiser*	*advertising, advertisement*
deport	*deportee*	*deportation*

(10 marks)

Test 72

72.1
1 motherhood	4 politeness	7 warmth	9 popularity
2 disagreement	5 reduction	8 friendliness	10 combination
3 apprenticeship	6 wisdom		

(10 marks)

72.2
1 relationship	5 improvement	9 achievements
2 sensitivity	6 expectations	10 curiosity
3 retirement	7 neighbourhood	11 partnership
4 kindness	8 stardom	12 freedom

(12 marks)

72.3 **pleasant:** [faith], calm, companionship, affection, generosity, humour, luck
unpleasant: boredom, carelessness, fear, frustration, hostility, laziness, rage (13 marks)

Test 73

73.1
1 top	3 free	5 proof	7 hand	9 up
2 absent	4 world	6 two	8 so	10 out

(10 marks)

73.2 air-conditioned rooms; first-hand knowledge; open-necked shirt; all-out strike; cut-price goods; long-standing relationship; long-distance runner; well-off middle classes; built-up areas; off-peak travel (10 marks)

73.3
1 open-toed shoes	3 a tight-fitting skirt
2 a big-headed person	4 a suntanned girl

5 a time-consuming job   **7** an interest-free loan
6 a broad-shouldered man   (7 marks)

73.4 **1** T
       2 F: a brand-new car is simply a very new one. It may or may not be revolutionary in design.
       3 T
       4 F: a self-centred person is someone who is always thinking of themselves rather
          than other people.
       5 T
       6 F: a bad-tempered person is someone who is often cross and in a difficult mood.
       7 F: a full-time job is one which occupies all your working life, typically 40 hours
          a week, often 9 to 5 in an office.
       8 T   (8 marks)

Test 74

74.1 trademark; tea bag; hay fever; generation gap; package holiday; youth hostel; pocket money; mother tongue; mineral water; cotton wool   (10 marks)

74.2 **1** blood   **3** control   **5** race
       2 alarm   **4** food   (5 marks)

74.3 **1** stop   **3** penalty   **5** change   **7** barrier
       2 account   **4** state   **6** tax   **8** wipers   (8 marks)

74.4 **1** d   **3** c   **5** k   **7** j   **9** i   **11** l
       2 f   **4** h   **6** a   **8** m   **10** b   **12** e   (12 marks)

Test 75

75.1 **1** i   **2** f   **3** k   **4** b   **5** h   **6** a   **7** d   **8** j   **9** g   **10** c   (10 marks)

75.2 **1** out; out   **3** out; back   **5** out; up
       2 back; up   **4** over; out   (10 marks)

75.3 **1** workouts   **4** input   **7** dropouts   **9** printout
       2 feedback   **5** cutbacks   **8** takeover   **10** break-up
       3 outbreak   **6** breakdown   (10 marks)

75.4 **1** lay-by   **3** outlets   **5** turnover
       2 outset   **4** breakthrough   (5 marks)

Test 76

76.1 give and take; prim and proper; rant and rave; rough and ready; wine and dine; part and parcel; odds and ends; rack and ruin; leaps and bounds; pick and choose (10 marks)

76.2 **1** rough and ready   **6** part and parcel
       2 prim and proper   **7** wine and dine
       3 give and take   **8** rack and ruin
       4 rant and rave   **9** pick and choose
       5 leaps and bounds   **10** odds and ends   (10 marks)

76.3 **1** or   **2** but   **3** or   **4** or   **5** to   (5 marks)

76.4 **1** peace   **4** forth   **7** down   **9** white
       2 recreation **5** off   **8** about   **10** gentlemen
       3 there   **6** give   (10 marks)

Test 77

77.1
1 Central Intelligence Agency
2 World Health Organisation
3 by the way
4 for your information
5 automated teller machine
6 North Atlantic Treaty Organisation
7 as far as I know
8 Military Intelligence 6
9 in my honest / humble opinion
10 away from keyboard   (10 marks)

77.2
1 science fiction
2 gigabyte
3 high-technology
4 university
5 air conditioning
6 satellite navigation system
7 mobile phone
8 carbohydrates   (8 marks)

77.3
1 Please get in touch *asap*.
2 We prefer to avoid *GM* foods.
3 The discovery of *DNA* has had a major impact on medical science.
4 Don't forget to take some kind of *ID* with you to the exam tomorrow.
5 It's the second time this year that James has gone *AWOL*.
6 Banks usually advise customers to memorise and not write down their *PINs*.
7 People in northern countries are more likely to suffer from *SAD*.
8 The police would like to interview anyone with any knowledge of the whereabouts of Sarah Lane, *aka* Sarah Fisher.
9 You may find the information you need on our *FAQ* webpage.   (9 marks)

77.4
1 as a word: /ˈleɪzə/
2 as individual letters or as full words: *Be right back.*
3 as letters: /aɪ ˈdiː/
4 as a word: /ˈreɪdɑː/
5 as a word: /ˈeɪwɒl/
6 usually as individual letters: /eɪ.es.eɪ.piː/ (but it may occasionally be heard as a word /ˈeɪ.sæp/)
7 in full: *see you later*
8 usually in full as either *Laughing out loud* or *Lots of love* or occasionally either as letters /el.əʊ.el/ or as a word: /lɒl/.   (8 marks)

Test 78

78.1
1 k   3 f   5 a   7 c   9 b
2 e   4 h   6 i   8 j   10 d   (10 marks)

78.2
1 stick   3 heavy   5 days   7 weight   9 dumps
2 barking 4 move   6 weather 8 red   10 gold   (10 marks)

78.3
1 is barking 3 made   5 under 7 brush 9 on
2 has seen   4 takes 6 meal   8 nose   10 pulling   (10 marks)

78.4
1 well-behaved
2 sit down
3 happy
4 difficult
5 They've got hold of the wrong end of the stick.   (5 marks)

Test 79

79.1
1 doubt   3 recipe   5 ought   7 sword   9 lamb
2 knee   4 cupboard 6 fasten   8 catastrophe 10 salmon   (10 marks)

79.2
1 lorry   3 bend   5 root   7 jerk
2 glove   4 room   6 walk   8 pain   (8 marks)

79.3 1 What are your country's main **exports**?
2 They have **conflicting** ideas about their own roles.
3 The children have made a lot of **progress** with their maths.
4 The value of property usually in**creases** every year.
5 Will they per**mit** you to work there?
6 Although he's Russian, he has a UK permanent residence **permit**.
7 The highest July temperatures in London ever were re**cord**ed today.
8 'I'll never de**sert** you,' the poet promised his beloved.
9 There is going to be an organised **protest** about the new by-pass.
10 What an **insult**! You have no right to speak to me like that.   (10 marks)

79.4 She left the pretty com**b** I gave her for Christ**m**as in the cas**t**le when we spent
an **h**our there last week. She took it out of her bag because she wanted to get
some **k**nots out of her hair after we'd been wa**l**king outside in the wind. Then
she must have dropped it. Luckily, an **h**onest person picked it up and took it back
to the information desk.
(Note that in some accents of English [e.g. those spoken in southern England,
Australia, etc.] /r/ may not be pronounced if it is not followed by a vowel sound,
e.g. at the end of *her, hour, after,* or in the middle of *person* and *information.*
These silent r's are not highlighted in this exercise.)   (7 marks)

Test 80

80.1

1 h		3 a		5 d		7 i		9 f	
2 j		4 g		6 c		8 e		10 b	(10 marks)

80.2

1 mash		4 groaned		7 dash		9 click	
2 splashing		5 clanging		8 whistle		10 grumbled	
3 clip-clopping		6 sprinkled					(10 marks)

80.3

1 smash		4 grumpy		7 wheeze		10 meow	
2 growl		5 spit		8 whizz		11 roar	
3 gash		6 moo		9 click			(11 marks)

80.4

1 d		2 a		3 e		4 b	(4 marks)

Test 81

81.1 Some possible answers:
be is a homophone of *bee*
lead is a homograph of the verb *to lead*
seen is a homophone of *scene*
like is a homograph of the verb *to like*
read is a homograph of the infinitive form *to read* and a homophone of *red*
size is a homograph of *sighs*
there is a homophone of *they're* and *their*
two is a homophone of *to* and *too*
row is a homograph of *row* (line) and a homophone of the verb *to row*
rolls is a homophone of *roles* and a homograph of (bread) *rolls*
live is a homograph of the adjective *live* (performance)
need is a homophone of the verb *to knead*
pen is a homograph of *pen* (for writing)
house is a homograph of the noun *house*   (10 marks)

81.2

1 weather / whether		4 break / brake		7 air / heir		9 sum / some	
2 our / hour		5 fare / fair		8 meet / meat		10 mail / male	
3 flu / flew		6 grown / groan					(10 marks)

81.3 1 *Tee* is a golfing term (= the little cup the golf ball rests on) and *tea time* is
  an everyday phrase.
  2 *Love at first sight* is an everyday phrase and *a site* is a place where an archaeological
  dig takes place.
  3 *Place* and *soul* are homophones of two types of fish, *plaice* and *sole*. A *fishmonger*
  sells fish.
  4 *Sale of the century* is a familiar phrase used to describe a spectacular sales event in
  a shop. *Sail* means travel in a boat.
  5 *And so on* is an everyday phrase. A *wardrobe mistress* sews costumes for actors.   (5 marks)

81.4 1 grinned   3 I've   5 so   7 spooned   9 now
  2 found   4 cows   6 nose   8 choose; juice   (10 marks)

Test 82

82.1 1 currency – uncountable   6 information – uncountable
  2 luggage – uncountable   7 travel – uncountable
  3 reservation – countable   8 visa – countable
  4 accommodation – uncountable   9 journey – countable
  5 flight – countable   10 transport – uncountable   (10 marks)

82.2 1 We're going to the shops tomorrow. I want to look at some new ~~furnitures~~ *furniture*.
  Maria wants to choose some skiing ~~equipments~~ *equipment* and Mei needs some ~~papers~~
  paper for her printer. We'll probably spend lots of ~~moneys~~ *money*.
  2 After doing courses at school, Sanjiv found that he was making ~~progesses~~ *progress*
  and increasing his ~~knowledges~~ *knowledge* of geography. He looked forward
  to continuing his studies at university and perhaps, one day, doing some ~~researches~~
  research into the geography of his local area.
  3 I really need some ~~advices~~ *advice* from you, as someone with a lot of ~~experiences~~
  experience, before I take up the violin. Do you have any tips about buying an
  instrument? Are there any works by famous composers that are easy for
  a beginner? What kinds of ~~musics~~ *music* would you recommend?   (10 marks)

82.3 bread; butter; flour; soup; spaghetti   (5 marks)

82.4 1 research   4 leather; – (= no article)   7 currency
  2 software   5 weather   8 some
  3 wealth   6 accommodation   9 some   (10 marks)

Test 83

83.1 binoculars; trousers; sunglasses; traffic lights; tongs; tweezers; pyjamas; shears;
  swimming trunks; overalls   (10 marks)

83.2 1 glasses   4 pliers   7 handcuffs   9 (kitchen) scales
  2 knickers / pants   5 scissors   8 headphones   10 braces
  3 goggles   6 shorts   (10 marks)

83.3 1 is   4 is; is; it   7 are going   9 are; they are
  2 was   5 are   8 is   10 are; ones
  3 is; it   6 was / is; it   (10 marks)

83.4 1 acoustics   2 authorities   3 contents   4 whereabouts   5 goods   (5 marks)

Test 84

84.1 1 (some) glass   4 fish; chicken   7 a chicken
  2 cloth   5 an iron   8 (any / some) paper
  3 a chocolate   6 a wood   9 glasses   (10 marks)

84.2
1 works	4 arts	7 peoples	
2 hairs	5 times; experiences	8 art	
3 people	6 Time	9 work	(10 marks)

84.3
1 *Pepper* is a spicy powder that you sprinkle on food (often with salt); *a pepper* is a type of vegetable.
2 *Iron* is a type of metal; *an iron* is something you press your clothes with to make them smooth.
3 *Plant* is used to describe large heavy machinery; *a plant* is something that grows in the earth.
4 *Coffee* is the general word for a type of drink; *a coffee* is a cup of coffee.
5 *Damage* means *harm* or *injury*; *damages* means money paid in compensation. (10 marks)

84.4
1 a piece of material to wipe something with
2 an eraser, something to rub out a written mistake
3 a piece from a bar of chocolate
4 some individual chocolates from a box
5 a piece of paper to write on (5 marks)

Test 85

85.1
1 lump	4 stroke	7 spots	
2 loaves; carton	5 breath	8 puff	
3 gust	6 articles	9 means	(10 marks)

85.2
Before you visit England, let me give you some *bits / pieces of advice* and some *pieces / bits of information*. Don't take too *many pieces of luggage* with you but take some warm *items / articles of clothing*. You never know whether you are going to get *a spell of good weather* or not. One day, you will have *claps / rumbles of thunder, flashes of lightning* and *spots / showers of rain* and the next it will be sunny. (8 marks)

85.3
1 state of emergency	4 state of poverty	6 state of flux	
2 state of disrepair	5 state of health	7 state of tension	
3 state of uncertainty			(7 marks)

85.4
1 blade	3 cloud	5 flash; clap	7 spell	
2 slices	4 bars; tube	6 stroke	8 items	(10 marks)

Test 86

86.1
1 flock; herd	3 swarm	5 gang; team	7 cast	
2 shoals	4 Packs	6 crowd; group		(10 marks)

86.2
1 a clump of trees; a range of mountains	4 a set of drums
2 a stack of chairs	5 a row of houses
3 a pile of books	(6 marks)

86.3
1 The staff are mostly young people.
2 The crew remained calm during the emergency landing.
3 The public have a right to know how government spends their taxes.
4 The team were congratulated by the captain.
5 The cast were just ordinary people, not famous actors.
6 The company are on strike and so there will be no performances. (6 marks)

86.4
1 a pile / heap of clothes	8 a group of islands
2 a set of glasses	9 a bunch of bananas
3 a flock of birds	10 a pile of dishes
4 a pair of shoes	11 a team of experts
5 a couple of apples	12 a stack of logs
6 a pack of (playing) cards	13 a set of pots and pans
7 a shoal of mackerel	(13 marks)

Test 87

87.1
1 a pail / bucket   5 a jug   8 a basket
2 a pan / saucepan   6 a sack   9 a barrel
3 a bowl   7 a mug   10 a jar
4 a tin / can   (10 marks)

87.2
1 *A bottle of milk* is a glass or plastic container usually holding a pint or litre of milk; *a crate of milk* is a plastic container which can hold twelve or twenty bottles of milk, making it easier for several bottles to be carried at once.
2 *A cup of tea* is what one person drinks; *a packet of tea* is what you buy in the shops and later open and use to make pots of tea.
3 *A box of sweets* is a cardboard container holding sweets; *a jar of sweets* is a glass or plastic container with a lid, which is filled with loose sweets.
4 *A shopping bag* is soft and can be folded up when not in use; *a shopping basket* is stiff, and often made of cane or metal (in a supermarket).
5 *A carton of juice* is a waterproof cardboard or plastic container holding juice which you buy from a shop; *a jug of juice* is a glass container that you can pour juice from into individual glasses.
6 *A pot of ointment* is a round jar into which you dip your finger when you want to use some ointment; *a tube of ointment* has to be squeezed to get the ointment out.
7 At home or in a restaurant you eat *a bowl* (usually ceramic) *of ice cream*; in a shop or at the cinema you can buy *a tub* (cardboard or plastic) *of ice cream*.
8 *A case of wine* is a box containing twelve bottles of wine; *a glass of wine* is an individual drink of wine.
9 *A packet of cards* is a set of, e.g. six greetings cards sold together; *a pack of cards* means a set of 52 playing cards.   (18 marks – 2 marks per question)

87.3
a box of: [paperclips], chocolates, tools, matches, tea bags
a jar of: honey, instant coffee, olives   (7 marks)

Test 88

88.1
1 *do* your homework   6 *do* the housework
2 *make* fun of something or someone   7 *make* a suggestion
3 *do* the cooking   8 *make* a profit
4 *do* an exercise   9 *do* business
5 *make* a good impression   10 *make* a success of something   (10 marks)

88.2
1 off   3 up for (2 marks)   5 without   7 of
2 up   4 for   6 out   8 up   (9 marks)

88.3
1 Have you done all your ~~homeworks~~ *homework* yet?
2 Try not to ~~do~~ *make* too many careless mistakes in your arithmetic test.
3 I've got a lot of work to ~~make~~ *do* this evening.
4 It's not easy to make a ~~going~~ *go* of a new business these days.
5 Can I help you ~~make~~ *do* the washing-up?
6 Mateusz has made the ~~arrangement~~ *arrangements* for our trip to Japan.   (6 marks)

88.4
1 made a loss   5 make allowances   8 do the gardening
2 make a noise   6 do the cooking   9 make a cup of tea
3 making the best of   7 make a decision   10 making a fuss
4 do your best   (10 marks)

Test 89

89.1
1 The government has promised to <u>bring down</u> petrol prices soon. *reduce*
2 Rachel <u>takes after</u> her mother in looks but her father in temperament. *resembles*
3 The scandal may well <u>bring down</u> the government. *destroy*
4 I wonder if they will ever <u>bring back</u> corporal punishment. *re-introduce*

5 Don't be <u>taken in</u> by his easy charm. He's got a cruel streak.   *deceived*
6 The difficulties suffered during the war eventually <u>brought about</u> a revolution.   *caused*
7 They're <u>bringing out</u> a new version of their mobile phone next month.   *introducing, producing, releasing*
8 She's trying to <u>bring</u> her husband <u>round</u> to the idea of moving to Rome.   *persuade*
9 Adam wishes he could <u>take back</u> his angry words.   *withdraw, retract*
10 We <u>took to</u> each other at once and speak on the phone almost daily now.   *liked*   (10 marks)

89.2
1 It's right that this affair should be brought into the open.
2 I hope they won't take advantage of you.
3 The research brought some interesting facts to light.
4 His rudeness took my breath away.
5 You must take applicants' experience as well as their qualifications into consideration.
6 I always took it for granted that you'd become a lawyer like your parents.
7 The new laws will soon be brought into force.
8 Going out on your own at this time of night is taking a risk.
9 Rick immediately started taking control of the situation.
10 It's hard to take Dan's ideas seriously.   (10 marks)

89.3
1 off	4 out	7 up	10 on	13 off
2 on	5 in	8 in	11 to	14 over / on
3 for	6 off	9 in	12 round	15 off (15 marks)

Test 90

90.1
1 c	3 j	5 h	7 k	9 e
2 f	4 a	6 b	8 d	10 g (10 marks)

90.2
1 bought	4 understand	7 prepare; buy
2 travelling	5 find, obtain	8 made the acquaintance of / met; become
3 become	6 annoys	(10 marks)

90.3
1 I wish I could get out *of* my dental appointment tomorrow! I hate having my teeth filled.
2 Unfortunately, Viktor and I ~~got to a bad start off~~ *got off to a bad start.*
3 I'm trying to think of a way to get ~~the~~ *my* own back on Dave for lying to me.
4 You obviously got out of bed on the ~~left~~ *wrong* side today!
5 We're ~~getting very well on with~~ *getting on very well with* the project now.   (5 marks)

90.4
1 down	4 up	7 across	9 on
2 get-together	5 behind	8 round	10 down
3 over	6 on		(10 marks)

Test 91

91.1
1 is being very firm
2 trying to force
3 made it his ambition to become
4 talking about how to solve important social problems
5 end
6 abandon, ignore
7 focus on, direct all his thoughts to
8 start
9 communicate this
10 irritated them   (10 marks)

91.2
1 set	3 set	5 set	7 put	9 set
2 put	4 put	6 set	8 set	(9 marks)

91.3
1 forward	3 aside	5 up	7 in	9 up
2 off	4 away	6 off	8 out	(9 marks)

91.4
1 put up with
2 put [you] off
3 put [this bookcase] together
4 set out

5 put [others] down
6 put up
7 put on

(7 marks)

Test 92

92.1
| 1 go | 3 goes | 5 came | 7 came | 9 came |
| 2 come | 4 went | 6 goes | 8 went | 10 go |

(10 marks)

92.2
1 make a success
2 separate
3 found
4 do anything

5 continuing
6 busy
7 getting a contract

8 within its limitations
9 are enthusiastic about
10 become fashionable

(10 marks)

92.3 **come to:** a decision; a standstill; an end; a conclusion
come into: [fashion], contact with; a fortune; view; existence; operation; sight (10 marks)

92.4
1 Milly has ~~come with up~~ *come up with* some very good ideas for the party.
2 I wouldn't want to ~~go such a terrible experience through~~ *go through such a terrible experience* again.
3 The boss is always ~~going at me on~~ *going on at me* about my untidy desk.
4 Would you like to ~~come to my house round~~ *come round to my house* this evening?
5 I hope the proposal will ~~go without any problems through~~ *go through without any problems.*

(5 marks)

Test 93

93.1
| 1 looking | 3 saw | 5 run | 7 turned | 9 broke |
| 2 run | 4 looked | 6 see | 8 let | 10 break |

(10 marks)

93.2
1 on the bright side
2 take turns at
3 over a new leaf
4 looks down on

5 break the news
6 let off
7 broke the record
8 seeing things

9 in the long run
10 broke her heart

(10 marks)

93.3
1 petrol, sugar
2 a party, a holiday
3 an invitation, a job

4 professional sportsmen and women, firefighters
5 news, promises

(10 marks)

93.4
1 Yes, they do; they like a big audience.
2 No, you mean that they are imagining that they can see something.
3 No, it usually means that you meet them unexpectedly.
4 At an airport or bus / railway station.
5 No, it has just been revealed as a fake – perhaps people initially thought it was genuine or perhaps they just weren't sure.

(5 marks)

Test 94

94.1
formal: [goodbye], go amiss, offspring, abode
neutral: bye-bye, go wrong, children, house
informal: cheerio, go pear-shaped, kids

(10 marks)

94.2 immediately – right away; seek – look for; fundamental – basic; occur – happen; frequently – often; utilise – use; establish – show; provide – give (8 marks)

94.3
1 The subway is closed until ~~furthest~~ *further* ~~notices~~ *notice*.
2 Do not ~~adress~~ *address* the driver unless the bus is ~~stationery~~ *stationary*.
3 Do not ~~alighten~~ *alight* while the bus is in ~~moving~~ *motion*.
4 Articles ~~deposed~~ *deposited* here must be paid for ~~on~~ *in* advance.
5 We regret ~~not longer~~ *we no longer* ~~to accept~~ *accept* cheques. (10 marks)

94.4   1 with   2 In; of   3 to   4 on   5 on; of   (7 marks)

Test 95

95.1
MONEY: dosh, readies
FOOD AND DRINK: [bread], cuppa, grub, nosh
JOBS: quack, squaddie, the bill
COMPUTER ENTHUSIASTS: anorak, nerd   (10 marks)

95.2
1 lab	3 mobile	5 mag	7 ad(vert)	9 paper
2 celeb	4 fridge	6 telly	8 vet	10 bike (10 marks)

95.3
1 in prison   4 five pounds
2 some potatoes   5 police officers
3 by underground   6 telephoning for a taxi   (6 marks)

95.4
1 vet	3 nosh	5 anorak	7 loo	9 dosh
2 ads	4 cuppa	6 mobile	8 cops	(9 marks)

Test 96

96.1
1 drunk	3 deaf	5 iron	7 ox	9 bold
2 mad	4 horse	6 bone	8 fish	10 bull (10 marks)

96.2
1 Yes, they were as good as gold.   4 No, he's as quiet as a mouse.
2 No, he's as sober as a judge.   5 Yes, she's as light as a feather.
3 Yes, he went as red as a beetroot.   (5 marks)

96.3
1 I slept very well.   6 Our plan worked very smoothly and well.
2 He vomited all night.   7 My father has very sharp eyes.
3 The goalkeeper was very upset and   8 Steve's in a bad mood.
   disappointed.   9 I forget everything / I've got a bad
4 She went very pale.   memory.
5 The lady's hands were very pale   10 She has a very big appetite / She eats a lot.
   and fair-skinned.   (10 marks)

96.4
1 She's as thin as a rake but as strong as an ox. (2 marks)
2 He's like a bear with a sore head today.
3 He's got a mind like a sieve and is as mad as a hatter. (2 marks)
4 His grandmother has got eyes like a hawk.
5 She looked as cool as a cucumber even though it was 30° in the shade.
6 My plan worked like a dream and the work was done as quick as a flash. (2 marks)
7 Party political broadcasts on TV are like a red rag to a bull for my dad. (10 marks)

Test 97

97.1
1 book; cover   3 cooks; broth   5 bridge
2 horse; water; drink   4 glass; throw   (10 marks)

97.2
1 Don't put all your ~~apples~~ *eggs* in one basket.   i
2 When the cat's away the ~~dogs~~ *mice* will play.   c
3 Never look a gift horse in the ~~eyes~~ *mouth*.   g

4 There's no smoke without ~~cigarettes~~ *fire*.   h
5 Many ~~fingers~~ *hands* make light work.   j
6 Take care of the pennies and the ~~dollars~~ *pounds* will take care of themselves.   b
7 One swallow doesn't make a ~~spring~~ *summer*.   e
8 Never judge a book by its ~~writer~~ *cover*.   d
9 Too many cooks spoil the ~~dinner~~ *broth*.   f
10 We'll cross that ~~street~~ *bridge* when we come to it.   a   (20 marks)

97.3 **1** People who live in glass houses shouldn't throw stones.
2 There's no smoke without fire.
3 You can lead a horse to water but you can't make it drink.
4 We'll cross that bridge when we come to it.
5 When the cat's away, the mice will play.   (5 marks)

Test 98

98.1 **1** on a road; Drivers must drive more slowly now.
2 on a cigarette packet; This product is harmful for your health.
3 in a car park; Drivers must buy a ticket from a machine that will allow them to park and put it where it can be seen behind their windscreens.
4 on some private land; People who go onto this land without permission will be taken to court.
5 at a place of entertainment; People under 18 will not be allowed in unless they are with an adult.   (10 marks)

98.2
1 c	**3** i	**5** h	**7** d	**9** a	**11** b
2 g	**4** l	**6** j	**8** f	**10** k	(11 marks)

98.3 **1** *Feeding the animals is strictly prohibited.* You must not give the animals any food.
2 *Place your purchases here.* Put the items you have bought here.
3 *No through road for motor vehicles.* This is a dead-end for cars.
4 *Kindly refrain from using mobile phones in the auditorium.* Please do not use mobile phones in the theatre / cinema / concert hall.
5 *Do not alight from the bus whilst it is in motion.* Don't get off the bus until it has stopped.
6 *Shoplifters will be prosecuted.* People who steal from the shop will be taken to court.
7 *Admission to ticket holders only.* You are not allowed to come in without a ticket.
(14 marks – 1 mark for the correct order and 1 for the correct meaning)

Test 99

99.1
1 BOOST encourage	**5** HIT affect	**9** PLOY clever activity
2 WED marry	**6** BLAZE fire	**10** BID attempt
3 STRIFE conflict	**7** PLEA request	
4 GO-AHEAD approval	**8** VOW promise	(10 marks)

99.2
1 supports; steps towards (peace)	**5** jewellery; manager
2 survey	**6** promises; take over (father's) job
3 discussions	**7** promises; reductions
4 dramatic situation	**8** possible losses / potential cut (12 marks)

99.3
1 an explosion at a factory	**5** They are puzzled by it.
2 jewels	**6** There was some kind of dispute or conflict.
3 help of some kind – financial or food, perhaps	**7** those workers with an essential role
4 difficult	**8** It is being / going to be restricted.

(8 marks)

99.4
1 *Axed* here means *dismissed* but an *axe* is a tool used to chop down a tree.
2 *Links* here means *connection* but *golf links* is a term for the place where the game of golf is played.
3 *Bar* here means *prohibition* but a *chocolate bar* is a large piece of chocolate.
4 *Drive* here means *campaign* but people also *drive* on roads.
5 *Curbed* here means *controlled* but *curb* sounds the same as *kerb* (the edge of the pavement i.e. the place where traffic wardens do a lot of their work). (5 marks)

Test 100

100.1

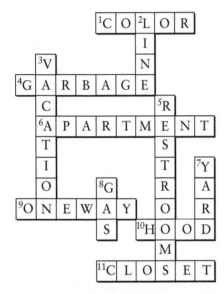

(10 marks)

100.2
1 nappy (Br) / diaper (US)
2 queue (Br) / line (US)
3 curtains (Br) / drapes (US)
4 rubber (Br) / eraser (US)
5 torch (Br) / flashlight (US)
6 lorry (Br) / truck (US)
7 tights (Br) / pantyhose (US)

(7 marks)

100.3
1 *wash up*: (a) wash the dishes (b) wash (your) hands
2 *first floor*: (a) floor above the ground floor, i.e. up one flight of stairs (b) ground floor, the floor on the same level as the street
3 *vest*: (a) undershirt (b) sleeveless garment worn over a shirt
4 *subway*: (a) underpass under a road (b) underground railway
5 *bill*: (a) piece of paper saying how much needs to be paid in a restaurant (b) banknote / piece of paper money (10 marks)

100.4
1 cookie
2 parking lot
3 sidewalk
4 Scotch tape
5 candy
6 round trip
7 crosswalk
8 elevator

(8 marks)